Manual
on the Character
and Fitness
Process for Application
to the Michigan State Bar

Law and Practice

Timothy A. Dinan

authorHOUSE®

AuthorHouse™ LLC
1663 Liberty Drive
Bloomington, IN 47403
www.authorhouse.com
Phone: 1-800-839-8640

Published by AuthorHouse 08/26/2014

ISBN: 978-1-4969-3410-9 (sc)
ISBN: 978-1-4969-3409-3 (e)

Library of Congress Control Number: 2014914923

Any people depicted in stock imagery provided by Thinkstock are models,
and such images are being used for illustrative purposes only.
Certain stock imagery © Thinkstock.

This book is printed on acid-free paper.

Because of the dynamic nature of the Internet, any web addresses or links contained in this book may have changed
since publication and may no longer be valid. The views expressed in this work are solely those of the author and do
not necessarily reflect the views of the publisher, and the publisher hereby disclaims any responsibility for them.

Table of Contents

Disclaimer

This manual is intended to provide general information about legal topics and should not be construed as legal advice. For specific questions regarding any legal matter, please consult your attorney.

Preface

This manual is to provide the reader with practical insights regarding the application and licensing process for those who wish to practice law in Michigan. I have attempted to provide citations for the outline regarding the Affidavit of Personal History, meetings with the District Committee, formal hearings before the SBM Standing Committee and formal hearings before the Board of Law Examiners.

Though I have conducted a great deal of research and sought feedback from other attorneys, I do not claim this volume is an encyclopedic endeavor, nor is it complete. I invite you, the reader, to provide comments, questions and any changes you believe would benefit a future edition of this manual.

Acknowledgments

Many people have assisted me in developing this manual. Many other people have directly or indirectly provided assistance through their advice and counsel. Having said that, I am indebted to my legal assistant, Karen Van Hook, who has the unenviable task of transcribing and editing the text; my friend and co-instructor, Sheila Garin, Esq., whose insights have sophisticated and improved this manual immensely; and to my former student and current collaborator, Michael Naughton, Esq., whose technical expertise helped me spread my message. I would also like to acknowledge all members of District Committees and the Standing Committee; Timothy Raubinger, Jana Benjamin, Sonia Allen and the entire Michigan Board of Law Examiners; the investigative staff and attorneys at the State Bar of Michigan and the many attorneys whose good examples and practical advice were part of my learning process in defining character and fitness in myself and others.

I also wish to thank my editors, Amy Petersen and Daphne Johnson, Esq., who carefully read the proposed transcripts and did a wonderful job clarifying the text and focusing the manual. Their changes and patience are invaluable.

I would be remiss if I did not acknowledge my wife, Julie, and my children, Tim, Mike and Claire, who challenge me every day to show my best character and fitness as a husband, father and professional.

Prologue

Character – the willingness to
accept responsibility for one's
own life – is the source from
which self respect springs
-Joan Didion

No matter what we have come
through, or how many perils
we have safely passed, or how
many imperfect and jagged –
in some places perhaps –
irreparably – our life has been,
we cannot in our heart of
hearts imagine how it could
have been different. As we look
back on it, it slips in behind us
in orderly array, and, with all
its mistakes, acquires a sort of eternal fitness,
and even, at times, of poetic glamour.
-Randolph Bourne

Chapter One

Defining Character and Fitness

INTRODUCTION

The legal profession in Michigan has a unique system of admitting and regulating its members. Unlike many occupations, attorneys are self-regulating and, to a certain extent, self-selective.[1] A number of histories have examined how American attorneys in training (clerks), following the English tradition, would intern with other attorneys to study the law with mentors. When clerks were deemed ready, they were presented to the local bench and bar who decided whether the apprentice had met the standard for practice, thus "passing the bar," the physical barrier dividing the front of the court from the rear. It was both literal and figurative.

The modern system has taken the licensure of attorneys from these local bars to statewide uniform administration of applications, uniform vetting of credentials and due process. All states have regulations regarding attorney admissions though there are as many systems and standards as there are states and territories.

Though similar to some professions, the legal profession nonetheless has unique characteristics that set it apart from many other professions. Like all jurisdictions, the State Bar of Michigan follows a traditional review of the applicant's credentials; however, Michigan also has requirements that set it apart.[2]

LEGAL BASIS

There are a number of sources that provide standards for admission to practice in Michigan. These include guides published by the State Bar of Michigan (SBM), classes and seminars held in Michigan law schools and numerous on-line sources for admissions data. However, the best place to start is to examine Michigan Compiled Laws. Statutorily, MCL 600.934 sets forth the standard for applicants to meet regarding fitness and good moral character. It states:

---

[1] In the wake of Sen. Arlan Meekhof's 2014 introduction of SB 743 which would allow attorneys to practice law in Michigan without joining the State Bar, the Michigan Supreme Court, on February 13, 2014, announced the creation of a task force to investigate this issue taking into account attorneys' First Amendment Rights and the need to regulate the legal profession.

[2] See also the Rules Concerning the State Bar of Michigan, Rule 15 - Admission to the Bar.

600.934 Qualifications for admission to bar; "good moral character" defined; election to use multi-state bar examination scaled score; disclosure of score.

Sec. 934.

(1) A person is qualified for admission to the bar of this state who proves to the satisfaction of the board of law examiners that he or she is a person of good moral character, is 18 years of age or older, has the required general education, learning in the law, and fitness and ability to enable him or her to practice law in the courts of record of this state, and that he or she intends in good faith to practice or teach law in this state. Additional requirements concerning the qualifications for admission are contained in subsequent sections of this chapter. As used in this subsection, "good moral character" means good moral character as defined and determined under 1974 PA 381, MCL 338.41 to 338.47.

(2) A person may elect to use the multi-state bar examination scaled score that the person achieved on a multi-state bar examination administered in another state or territory when applying for admission to the bar of this state, but only if all of the following occur:

(a) The score that the person elects to use was achieved on a multi-state examination administered within the 3 years immediately preceding the multi-state bar examination in this state for which the person would otherwise sit.

(b) The person achieved a passing grade on the bar examination of which the multi-state examination the score of which the person elects to use was a part.

(c) The multi-state examination the score of which the person elects to use was administered in a state or territory that accords the reciprocal right to elect to use the score achieved on the multi-state examination administered in this state to Michigan residents seeking admission to the bar of that state or territory.

(d) The person earns a grade on the essay portion of the bar examination that when combined with the transferred multi-state scaled score constitutes a passing grade for that bar examination.

(e) The person otherwise meets all requirements for admission to the bar of this state.

(3) The state board of law examiners shall disclose to a person electing under subsection (2) to transfer the multi-state bar examination scaled score achieved on an examination administered in another state or territory the score the person achieved as soon as that score is received by the board regardless of whether the person could have obtained that score in the jurisdiction in which the examination was administered. This subsection does not require disclosure by the board of the score

achieved on a multi-state bar examination administered in another state or territory until the scores achieved on that examination administered in Michigan are released.

History: 1961, Act 236, Eff. Jan. 1, 1963;-- Am. 1972, Act 87, Imd. Eff. Mar. 20, 1972;-- Am. 1978, Act 289, Eff. July 10, 1978;-- Am. 1980, Act 271, Imd. Eff. Oct. 6, 1980;-- Am. 2000, Act 112, Imd. Eff. May 24, 2000;-- Am. 2004, Act 558, Imd. Eff. Jan. 3, 2005 Constitutionality: Requirement of United States citizenship as a necessary prerequisite for the admission to the practice of law constitutes denial of equal protection of the law under Const 1963, art I, § 2, and US Const, am XIV, § 1. In re Houlahan, 389 Mich 665; 209 NW2d 250 (1973), decided prior to the 1978 amendment.[3]

MCL 600.934(1) uses precise language to set forth its requirements. To practice law in Michigan, you must demonstrate to the satisfaction of the Board of Law Examiners that the applicant:

1. Is 18 years or older;
2. Has the required general education, learning in the law;
3. Has the fitness and ability to enable him or her to practice law in the courts of record in Michigan;
4. Intends in good faith to practice or teach law in Michigan; and
5. Possess 'good moral character'

These are not the only requirements. The Michigan Supreme Court, through the Board of Law Examiners, sets forth more specific requirements in terms of law school requirements, passing scores on the MPRE (Multistate Professional Responsibility Examination) and, of course, the Michigan Bar Examination.

GOOD MORAL CHARACTER

Section (1) references MCL 338.41 through 338.47 as to what constitutes "good moral character." MCL 338.41 states:

338.41 "**Good moral character**" and "**principal department**" **defined**.

Sec. 1.

(1) The phrase "good moral character", or words of similar import, when used as a requirement for an occupational or professional license or when used as a requirement to establish or operate an organization or facility regulated by this state in the Michigan Compiled Laws or administrative rules promulgated under those laws shall be construed to mean the **propensity on the part of the person** to serve the public in the licensed area in a fair, honest, and open manner. [Emphasis added.]

---

[3]   Michigan Legislative Website, www.legislature.mi.gov.

(2) As used in this act, "principal department" means the department which has jurisdiction over the board or agency issuing the license.

History: 1974, Act 381, Eff. Apr. 1, 1975;-- Am. 1978, Act 294, Imd. Eff. July 10, 1978 Compiler's Notes: For transfer of powers and duties of adult foster care licensing from the department of social services to the director of the department of commerce, see E.R.O. No. 1996-1, compiled at MCL 330.3101 of the Michigan Compiled Laws. For transfer of powers and duties of the bureau of family services from the department of consumer and industry services to the family independence agency by Type II transfer, see E.R.O. No. 2003-1, compiled at MCL 445.2011. (Id.)

For purposes of an application to practice law, the phrase, ". . . a propensity on the part of the person to serve the public in the licensed area in a <u>fair</u>, <u>honest</u>, and <u>open manner</u>." . . . defines the most important characteristics of what attorneys need to possess. While these terms may not have the same import for other professions, attorneys are officers of the court, agents of their clients as well as servants of their clients (albeit a paid servant). This implies fiduciary duties on a licensed attorney in regard to conduct not only with clients, but with the courts and the general public as well as in accordance with the Michigan Rules of Professional Conduct (MRPC) 1.8. Thus, the SBM looks for past conduct that, if still present, would hinder an applicant's ability to practice within these standards.

Such a broad and open definition allows for varying interpretations by applicants as well as SBM's Standing Committee and District Committee members. Phrases such as "protect the public" and "entrust to the public" are often used in committee hearings and seen in written opinions. These references relate back to that fundamental definition.

PRIOR CRIMINAL HISTORY

The second statute referenced in MCL 600.943 is MCL 338.42. This statute discusses the effect of a criminal conviction on an applicant who wishes to practice law. It holds:

338.42 Judgment of guilt in criminal prosecution or judgment in civil action as evidence in determining good moral character; notice; rebuttal.

Sec. 2.

A judgment of guilt in a criminal prosecution or a judgment in a civil action shall not be used, in and of itself, by a licensing board or agency as proof of a person's lack of good moral character. It may be used as evidence in the determination, and when so used the person shall be notified and shall be permitted to rebut the evidence by showing that at the current time he or she has the ability to, and is likely to, serve the public in a fair, honest, and open manner, that he or she is rehabilitated, or that the substance of the former offense is not reasonably related to the occupation or profession for which he or she seeks to be licensed. [Emphasis added.]

History: 1974, Act 381, Eff. Apr. 1, 1975;-- Am. 1978, Act 294, Imd. Eff. July 10, 1978 Compiler's Notes: For transfer of powers and duties of the bureau of family services from the department of consumer and industry services to the family independence agency by Type II transfer, see E.R.O. No. 2003-1, compiled at MCL 445.2011. (Ibid.)

Here, the effect of a criminal conviction or judgment in a civil action does not itself prevent one from being licensed. However, it does allow that the conviction to be used as evidence whether the applicant will conduct himself in a fair, honest and open manner. It allows for consideration of whether the person is rehabilitated, how the conviction is associated to the crime and whether that association/judgment affects the ability of the applicant to act in a fair, honest and open manner in the legal profession.

In a profession based in the law, it is a reasonable inquiry for SBM to know the facts of an arrest or a conviction. Sometimes, these revelations demonstrate isolated circumstances and anomalies in an otherwise normal history. Applicants often learn from these experiences and can demonstrate their maturation. Each incident is unique and must be considered in light of the applicant's complete history and circumstances. In instances of re-occurring or serial behaviors, the committee will look for a greater degree of effort in rehabilitation. Restitution and compliance with court orders are relevant as is conduct after court supervision is terminated.

The State Bar of Michigan Standing Committee on Character and Fitness Rules of Procedure (herein SBMCCF Rules) recognizes the provisions of this statute (See Appendix D – Rule E.3.).

For example, a homicide conviction may not necessarily be a bar to licensure where a fraud or theft conviction may be depending on the factors cited in the statute as well as those enumerated in the SBMCCF Rules. Each case will be individually considered in order for a panel to recommend whether it believes that the applicant has the requisite character and fitness.

In essence, an applicant must explain him or herself. This statute and the SBMCCF Rules provide a forum and a structure within which to do so. A more thorough explanation of how this is done is found in the SBMCCF Rules.

USE OF CRIMINAL RECORDS TO REVIEW APPLICANTS

MCL 338.43 discusses the use of criminal records in the examination process for an applicant seeking a license. Keep in mind these statutes apply to all professions, not just the legal profession. It states:

> 338.43 **Using, examining, or requesting certain criminal records prohibited; prerequisites for furnishing criminal records; rules**.
>
> Sec. 3.
>
> (1) The following criminal records shall not be used, examined, or requested by a licensing board or agency in a determination of good moral character when used as a requirement to establish or operate an organization or facility regulated by this state, or pursuant to occupational or professional licensure:

(a) Records of an arrest not followed by a conviction.

(b) Records of a conviction which has been reversed or vacated, including the arrest records relevant to that conviction.

(c) Records of an arrest or conviction for a misdemeanor or a felony unrelated to the person's likelihood to serve the public in a fair, honest, and open manner.

(d) Records of an arrest or conviction for a misdemeanor for the conviction of which a person may not be incarcerated in a jail or prison.

(2) A criminal record shall not be furnished to a licensing board or agency except by the principal department, and shall be furnished only after the director of the principal department or a person designated by the director has determined that the information to be provided to the board or agency meets the criteria set forth in this section.

(3) The director or a person designated by the director of the principal department shall promulgate rules for each licensing board or agency under that department's jurisdiction which prescribe the offenses or categories of offenses which the department considers indicate a person is not likely to serve the public as a licensee in a fair, honest, and open manner. Each licensing board or agency may make recommendations to the director regarding the rules to be promulgated. The rules shall be consistent with this act and promulgated pursuant to Act No. 306 of the Public Acts of 1969, as amended, being sections 24.201 to 24.315 of the Michigan Compiled Laws. Prior to the promulgation of the rules pertaining to a board or agency, all felonies shall be considered by the board or agency to be relevant to the ability or likelihood the person will serve the public in a fair, honest and open manner.

History: 1974, Act 381, Eff. Apr. 1, 1975;-- Am. 1978, Act 294, Imd. Eff. July 10, 1978 Compiler's Notes: For transfer of powers and duties of the bureau of family services from the department of consumer and industry services to the family independence agency by Type II transfer, see E.R.O. No. 2003-1, compiled at MCL 445.2011. (Ibid.)

Two questions on the Affidavit of Personal History deal with criminal convictions, expunged convictions, arrests and other matters seemingly barred by the above cited statute. Attorneys and applicants, having been trained in the law, are presumed to be knowledgeable of the law and its consequences. Because of the fiduciary role of attorneys, their access to sensitive data, the trust vested in attorneys by their status and license, and their roles as officers of the court, these matters are required to be disclosed to SBM as a routine part of the application. These records may indicate other problems such as substance abuse or mental illness.

There is no cited case law on the issue of an applicant's purposeful non-disclosure of an arrest not leading to a conviction, an expunged arrest, or a conviction that was set aside. However, it is helpful to note that:

> As an agent of the Board of Law Examiners, the State Bar of Michigan's Character and Fitness Committee conducts character and fitness investigations of each bar applicant. Thus, the Board of Law Examiners and the Character and Fitness Committee are designated and empowered to discharge the statutorily defined duties of the Michigan Supreme Court. *McCready v Michigan State Bar*, 881 F Supp 300, 303 (WD Mich, 1995); *Scullion v State Bd of Law Examiners*, 102 Mich App 711, 715; 302 NW2d 290 (1981).[4]

It appears that all the above-cited information would be considered necessary in determining whether an applicant has good moral character and will continue to be part of the inquiry. Some scholarly writings have addressed the subject of whether an expunged conviction should be a component of a Character & Fitness (C & F) investigation.

Understandably, any criminal conviction may be embarrassing and potentially bar admission to the State Bar for a few individuals. This data is important for the SBM to consider the nature of the conduct, whether a conviction was entered and whether a question would arise regarding the character of the applicant that could impact his or her character and fitness.

OTHER PUBLIC RECORDS

MCL 338.44 allows for the use of other public records to determine fitness for practice. The statute states:

> 338.44 **Use of public records or other sources to determine person's fitness**.
>
> Sec. 4.
>
> This act shall not bar the use by a licensing board or agency in its determination of a person's fitness, of any other public record, not related to arrest or prosecution, or of any other source of unbiased and accurate information.
>
> History: 1974, Act 381, Eff. Apr. 1, 1975; -- Am. 1978, Act 294, Imd. Eff. July 10, 1978 Compiler's Notes: For transfer of powers and duties of the bureau of family services from the department of consumer and industry services to the family independence agency by Type II transfer, see E.R.O. No. 2003-1, compiled at MCL 445.2011. (Ibid.)

The SBM requires both public and private records including employment records, school records, records from legal proceedings and relevant documents filed with government agencies to determine

---

[4]   *Nordman v State Bar of Michigan and Supreme Court of Michigan*, COA No. 209342, Unpublished opinion Otober 8, 1999.

fitness for licensure. This is not a catch-all statute, but rather recognition that if needed, the public and other records are available for review by SBM in order to fully assess the applicant's fitness.

These records potentially yield insight into more esoteric elements of the applicant's character. A history of being dismissed from jobs may demonstrate an applicant's inability to work with others or that he or she was the victim of workplace harassment. Either way, these records help SBM obtain a clearer picture of the applicant.

In short, the District Committee issues a written report and recommendation on each applicant interviewed which is then sent to the Standing Committee on Character and Fitness. After receiving the District Committee Report, the Standing Committee may:

1. 1) endorse the recommendation;
2. 2) take the recommendation under advisement pending additional information;
3. 3) remand the recommendation to the District Committee with instructions for further proceedings, or;
4. 4) reject the recommendation and conduct a hearing de novo at the request of the applicant.

All recommendations are ultimately transmitted to the Board of Law Examiners for final action.[5]

DUE PROCESS

MCL 338.45 provides for due process if an applicant is found unqualified for a license due to lack of good moral character or similar criteria. It provides:

> 338.45 **Finding person unqualified; statement; rehearing**.
>
> Sec. 5.
>
> When a person is found to be unqualified for a license because of a lack of good moral character, or similar criteria, the person shall be furnished by the board or agency with a statement to this effect. The statement shall contain a complete record of the evidence upon which the determination was based. The person shall be entitled, as of right, to a rehearing on the issue before the board if he or she has relevant evidence not previously considered, regarding his or her qualifications.
>
> History: 1974, Act 381, Eff. Apr. 1, 1975;-- Am. 1978, Act 294, Imd. Eff. July 10, 1978 Compiler's Notes: For transfer of powers and duties of the bureau of family services from the department of consumer and industry services to the family independence agency by Type II transfer, see E.R.O. No. 2003-1, compiled at MCL 445.2011. (Ibid.)

This statute corresponds with SBMCCF Rules for District Committee Meetings and Standing Committee Hearings as well as hearings before the Board of Law Examiners. All of the rules for these hearings are discussed in subsequent chapters of this book and are found in the [Appendices B & C]

---

[5]   State Bar of Michigan 2012-2013 Committee Annual Report.

It is important to note that the licensure process for applicants who may have character and fitness issues is not necessarily swift or certain despite provisions for time limits set forth in SBMCCF Rules or the Board of Law Examiners (BLE) rules.

Judicial Review of SBM/BLE Determinations

MCL 338.46 provides for judicial review for an aggrieved candidate. It states:

338.46 Judicial review; statement; order.

Sec. 6.

A person, aggrieved by a licensing agency or board determination regarding the person's possession of good moral character, if unsatisfied by his or her administrative appeal as provided in section 5, may bring an action in circuit court for a review of the record. If, in the opinion of the circuit court, the record does not disclose a lack of good moral character, as defined in this act, the court shall so state and shall order the board to issue the license, when all other licensing requirements are complied with.

History: 1974, Act 381, Eff. Apr. 1, 1975;-- Am. 1978, Act 294, Imd. Eff. July 10, 1978 Compiler's Notes: For transfer of powers and duties of the bureau of family services from the department of consumer and industry services to the family independence agency by Type II transfer, see E.R.O. No. 2003-1, compiled at MCL 445.2011. (Ibid.)

The authority to issue licenses to practice law comes from the Michigan Supreme Court. No matter what level of examination and scrutiny an applicant receives, the Board of Law Examiners reviews all applications whether routinely submitted (i.e. without any investigation beyond the initial Affidavit of Personal History) or submitted after favorable reviews from the District and/or Standing Committees. The BLE reserves the right to review all applications made to practice law and may request De Novo hearings even when the candidate has received positive determinations from the District and/or Standing Committee.[6]

The BLE promulgated its latest Rules for the Board of Law Examiners in September 2013 (See Appendix E). These rules are complementary to the SBMCCF procedures. Rule 2 addresses the requirements of good moral character. It also notes the availability of a hearing before the Board, which is addressed subsequently in this book. Rule 2 states:

Rule 2. Admission by Examination

"(A) An application must be filed by November 1 for the February examination, or March 1 for the July examination. Late applications will be accepted until December 15 for the February examination, or May 15 for the July examination. An application must be accompanied by payment of the fee. All materials filed are confidential.

---

[6]   See also MCL 600.922 and MCL 600.925.

(B) Before taking the examination, an applicant must obtain a JD degree from a reputable and qualified law school that

(1) is incorporated in the United States, its territories, or the District of Columbia; and

(2) requires for graduation 3 school years of study for full-time students, and 4 school years of study for part-time or night students. A school year must be at least 30 weeks.

A law school approved by the American Bar Association is reputable and qualified. Other schools may ask the Board to approve the school as reputable and qualified. In the event the law school has ceased operations since an applicant's graduation, the request for approval may be made by the applicant. The Board may in its discretion permit applicants who do not possess a JD degree from an ABA-approved law school to take the examination based upon factors including, but not limited to, relevant legal education, such as an LLM degree from a reputable and qualified law school, and experience that otherwise qualifies the applicant to take the examination.

(C) The State Bar character and fitness committee will investigate each applicant. The applicant must disclose any criminal conviction which carries a possible penalty of incarceration in jail or prison that has not been reversed or vacated and comply with the committee's requirements and requests. The committee will report the results of its investigation to the Board. If the committee report shows that an applicant lacks the necessary character and fitness, the Board will review the application, record, and report. If the Board accepts the report, the applicant is entitled to a hearing before the Board and may use the Board's subpoena power. The Board may permit an applicant to take the examination before the character and fitness committee reports. The Board will release the applicant's grade if character and fitness committee approval is obtained.

(D) Every applicant for admission must achieve a passing score, as determined by the Board, on the Multistate Professional Responsibility Examination.

(E) The Board may permit an applicant entering the armed forces before the examination immediately following graduation to take an earlier examination. The applicant must have completed, before the examination, 2 1/2 years full-time or 3 1/2 years part-time study. The Board will release the applicant's grade when the school certifies the applicant's graduation.

(F) The applicant is responsible for meeting all requirements before the examination. The Board may act on information about an applicant's character whenever the information is received." (Emphasis added)

Rule 2(C) provides for due process through the Board of Law Examiners that issues the license. If the applicant is further aggrieved by the findings of the BLE, s/he may file a writ of superintending control with the Michigan Supreme Court according to Rule 2(C)-3 of the BLE rules. Rule 2(C) states:

2(C)-1. <u>Duration of Character and Fitness Clearance.</u>

Character and fitness clearance is valid for three years. The three-year period begins with the exam first applied for by the applicant, regardless of when clearance is obtained and whether the applicant actually sat for that examination. For example, an applicant applying for the February 2005 examination and receiving character and fitness clearance, would need to be re-approved before being allowed to sit for the February 2008 examination. Applicants not passing the examination within three years after receiving clearance must again be approved by the State Bar Standing Committee on Character and Fitness.

2(C)-2. <u>Character and Fitness Hearings.</u> Character and fitness hearings are heard de novo. They are confidential proceedings. The applicant has the burden of proving by clear and convincing evidence that he or she has the requisite character and fitness to practice law. The Michigan Rules of Evidence are considered as guidelines but are not binding. If the parties agree, the hearing can be limited to an appeal consisting of briefs and argument or a limited testimonial hearing. All evidence is taken under oath before a court reporter, although the parties may stipulate to present testimony by telephone. The applicant may be represented by counsel.

2(C)-3. <u>Review of Board's Decision/Reapplication.</u> There are no motions for rehearing or reconsideration of decisions made following character and fitness hearings. Review is by complaint for superintending control filed in the Supreme Court. Applicants denied character and fitness certification by the Board may not reapply for certification for two years after the denial. The Board may extend that period to up to five years. In that case, the Board's opinion will specify the reasons for imposition of the longer time period. The Board may impose a waiting period shorter than two years. Applicants must reapply to the Standing Committee, not the Board.

Again, these rules are complementary to the SBMCCF procedures. These rules also set forth the period when a rejected applicant may reapply.

<u>Authority of Attorney Grievance Commission</u>

Finally, MCL 338.47 addresses the authority of the Attorney Grievance Commission (AGC) and the Attorney Discipline Board (ADB) to discipline licensees stating:

338.47 **Power to discipline licensees not affected**.

Sec. 7.

This act does not affect the power of a licensing agency to discipline licensees under its jurisdiction for prohibited acts of professional misconduct or dishonesty.

History: 1974, Act 381, Eff. Apr. 1, 1975 Compiler's Notes: For transfer of powers and duties of the bureau of family services from the department of consumer and industry services to the family independence agency by Type II transfer, see E.R.O. No. 2003-1, compiled at MCL 445.2011. (Ibid.)

The Attorney Grievance Commission has investigative authority over attorneys accused of violating the Michigan Rules of Professional Conduct (MRPC). Pursuant to Michigan Court Rule (MCR) 9.108(A) it is the prosecution arm of the Michigan Supreme Court. An issue that sometimes comes before the AGC includes matters regarding the attorney's affidavit of personal history that were not fully disclosed or were shaded in a manner raising suspicion requiring further inquiry. Undisclosed, shaded or misrepresented facts on the affidavit can subject an attorney to discipline. The Attorney Discipline Board is the adjudicative arm of the Michigan Supreme Court. Upon a finding of misconduct the ADB may revoke, suspend, reprimand, place on probation or issue no discipline regarding the license of the attorney at issue.

SUBJECTIVE BASIS

The interpretation of these rules in the application process is made by individuals. However their recommendation is made according to statute and rules based on specific facts of the matter before them with the goal of maintaining and preserving the good order of the profession and the law. Once the application process goes from a routine investigation to a referral to the District Committee or beyond, other elements necessarily come into play. The proceeding chapters in this manual address the impression that applicants make on their affidavit of personal history, in their District Committee Hearing and before the Standing Committee.

Everything said and done by the applicant in this process is subject to review. You cannot predict what issues may strike concern in an investigator or a committee member. Knowing this, it is always important to be respectful, forthright, patient and open. Ultimately, the applicant's efforts in this process will highlight your good character. Applicants need to be true to themselves, respect the process and be sensitive to the needs of your audience. These are skills all attorneys use every day in practice.

Chapter Two

THE SBM APPLICATION PROCESS

The longest journey is
the journey inward.
-Dag Hammarskjold

Life is a long lesson in humility.
-James M. Barrie

Chapter Two

The SBM Application Process

The application process for membership in the State Bar of Michigan can be lengthy and involved. For some, that is an understatement.

All applicants seek a license to practice law in Michigan. This license allows an attorney to give out legal advice, interpret laws and bring original actions within the court system. It is a license that exempts an individual from needing a separate real estate license. It permits someone to write checks out of a business account where checks are not always accepted. It is a license that does not involve an apprenticeship beyond what has already been performed in law school. A law license that has been held for twenty years has the same rights and privileges as one that was issued yesterday. The license makes you an officer of the court.

In other words, it is a powerful and all encompassing license. It vests both implied trust and status. Where law school can be referred to as the "Swiss Army Knife of Graduate Degrees," a law license is a ubiquitous business license. Many licensed attorneys do not practice law in the traditional sense, but rather, use their legal training in the business realm.

The applicant must carefully prepare their Affidavit of Personal History (APH) and accompanying documents to be submitted to the State Bar of Michigan. This is the basis upon which the applicant will be investigated, potential issues will be explored and further inquiries can be made. The Affidavit guides SBM as well as the applicant.

Unlike an application for a job or membership in an organization, joining the State Bar of Michigan as an attorney requires the applicant to swear out an oath regarding all the information provided. This means all facts represented in the APH, no matter how mundane, are true and accurate to the best of the affiant. This is no small feat when you consider all the details that could possibly encompass. Be cautioned however, that lack of facts on the AHP can also prove detrimental to the applicant. The information provided must be truthful and complete.

ADMISSION TO STATE BAR OF MICHIGAN

There are a number of ways one can be admitted to practice law in Michigan. These options all depend upon one's status when the APH is submitted.

A. Admission with Examination:

If the Applicant has not been previously licensed, then s/he will complete a new application and sit for Michigan's bar examination, offered on the last Tuesday and Wednesday of July and February. The applicant must complete the APH and have it filed timely with all fees paid. Once the APH is complete, the applicant may take the Michigan Bar Examination once prior to receiving clearance for character and fitness from the BLE. Any passing score is made official only after having received character and fitness clearance from the BLE.

B. Admission without Examination:

Attorneys, who have been previously licensed in other jurisdictions, may qualify to be admitted without taking an examination in Michigan. This would include attorneys who have been admitted to state bars whose licensing jurisdiction has reciprocity with Michigan. However, these attorneys still need to complete the character and fitness portion of the process, including the requisite APH and subsequent investigation. An attorney licensed in another jurisdiction may also be required to take and pass the MPRE if not previously taken.

Attached as an appendix (Appendix B) to this manual are the rules for the affidavit and various copies of forms. These rules should be followed precisely. Carelessness on the application will lead to your first problems with the character and fitness process. The most up-to-date forms and instructions are found at: http://www.michbar.org/professional/barexam.cfm

COMMON PROBLEMS IN THE APPLICATION PROCESS

1. Communicating:

The application is a two-way process. The applicant needs to be in communication with the State Bar of Michigan Character and Fitness Department as needed.

You should call,[7] mail or email the Character and Fitness Department if you have any questions or need clarification. The investigators and management team of the Character and Fitness Department are available to answer questions and assist applicants. Generally speaking, they are a frequently underutilized resource. The department regularly speaks at Michigan law schools along with representatives of the Board of Law Examiners. They stress the need to carefully prepare the APH and to review answers supplemented by documents.

There seems to be a perception that there is an adversarial relationship between the applicant and the State Bar of Michigan. I disagree. A great majority of applications are routinely handled without delay or issue. It only appears adversarial when the APH suggests the potential of a problem. Even then, the State Bar of Michigan graduates its scrutiny on an as needed basis.

2. Incomplete Affidavit:

---

[7]   **(517) 342-6400**

The most common problem is that of an incomplete APH submitted by the applicant. This means leaving out dates for jobs, failing to properly document where the applicant has lived, where s/he may have gone to school, etc.

As the State Bar of Michigan conducts its own independent investigation of the applicant, the applicant's information is considered to be the primary source for its investigation. Should the information turn out to be incorrect, false, misleading or lacking for any reason, the applicant's file will immediately be flagged for further review.

Further review is sometimes as simple as a letter of clarification. Perhaps there was a misspelling or misidentification. Perhaps the account number in question was transposed. Whatever the case may be, it is important to be precise. It is a human trait to err and, over a lifetime, the applicant may have forgotten some of life's details. However, it is the applicant's responsibility to review history and recreate an accurate accounting of facts.

A request to correct this information should be responded to as soon as possible. If you anticipate a delay in getting the requested information, let the State Bar of Michigan know, preferably before the time period for a response has expired. If you need help to get missing or incomplete information, ask for assistance. It is the applicant's responsibility to complete the APH, but that does not mean the SBM cannot be of assistance. The SBM website has guidelines and suggestions on how to track down information. You may want to seek out old tax returns, your social security records, school records, military records and other personal sources of your educational and work history. For applicants who are uncertain how to track down their own personal history, a private investigator has the tools to harness the public records to help the applicant find any and all relevant information.

3. Withholding Information:

Withholding information, any information, can lead to a lengthy, time consuming and angst-filled application review process. It is rarely the "crime," but always the "cover-up," so to speak, that sparks further investigation. Think about Watergate and its progeny.

Attorneys come from a broad spectrum of experiences and backgrounds. The trait common to all attorneys is their humanity. It is this same humanity that leads to youthful mistakes. It is immaturity, use of poor judgment, miscalculation, or misunderstandings which lead to consequences beyond the act itself. <u>One of the most important things an applicant must do in their application process is to be honest about prior mistakes on the APH</u>. In the long run, you are better off dealing with a disclosed matter than you are dealing with your honesty with an undisclosed matter that is subsequently discovered. Trying to sugarcoat past events or trying to save your ego from shame by misinformation and omission of information, is not recommended.

Many applicants ponder what they have to reveal about their past on the APH. Naturally, applicants want to put their best face forward. The APH has very specific directions about disclosing past conduct including suppressed convictions, expunged convictions, traffic misdemeanors, in-school discipline (e.g. within the dormitory or in-school discipline process) and related matters. The background investigation is designed to draw out this information whether the applicant reveals it or not. Again, take the time to carefully review the directions on the application and carefully consider your past. You are always better off disclosing information than leaving personal blemishes to be later discovered.

Let me reiterate this: be brutally honest and open about your prior mistakes, misfortunes, firings, errors, and plain stupidity, etc. This includes matters you may still be angry about or felt slighted by; this includes things which are seemly petty such as a number of parking tickets resulting in some enforcement action or a series of bounced checks (even checks covered by overdraft protection). Everybody brings their mistakes and shortcomings to the application process. You cannot escape your past nor should you. One of the most important things you will do as an applicant is to acknowledge your past transgressions and mistakes. The most obvious demonstration of current character is representing how you see these events, how you handled the incident(s) and grew from it/them.

4. Purposeful non-disclosure

Purposefully not disclosing a matter is a cardinal sin of the process. The application and its accompanying instructions make it entirely clear that an applicant <u>must</u> disclose all information. It is human nature to not want to disclose information that is embarrassing or might cast you in a negative light. However, you must disclose all matters, regardless of how trivial or embarrassing you may feel they are.

The choice to not disclose something and then have it arise later in the process is tantamount to guaranteeing at least a one-year delay in issuing a law license, if not other difficulties. Please be aware of that consequence.

a.*Misstatement or partial disclosure of a reported item*

Most applicants make disclosures on items for which they know they must provide a disclosure and explanation. Sometimes this disclosure is made in a partial manner or in a manner that attempts to cast the applicant's acts/efforts in a more favorable light. For instance, perhaps an applicant had a police incident where they were involved in a fight. The applicant's recollection of the fight may have changed since it happened. Nevertheless, there will be a further investigation into the matter, especially if the police were involved. If an applicant's version differs greatly from that of the police report, then it will be subject to further scrutiny by the Character and Fitness Committee. It is wise to review all documents related to an incident before committing to any facts on your APH regarding the incident being disclosed. An applicant can even acknowledge that there is another set of facts regarding the incident or make reference to the police report and where there may be differences. Nonetheless, to color the facts in an applicant's favor or to otherwise selectively document a reported incident will slow down the application process.

One of the best things to do when preparing your APH is to seek out as many records and cross-references as possible. Prior to the advent of widespread computer usage, applications could be held up for months because of the time it took for official records to be produced and verified. This is no longer the case. With instant communication, the power of the internet, and the availability of court records, tax records, driving records and credit records, all answers could be cross-referenced in at least one form. As an example, an applicant's social security records should be able to reflect every paid position they ever held while school records ought to be a reflection of at least some, if not all, externship records. A list of resources is available in Appendix C. As mentioned previously, a competent private investigator can assist in the production of public records and semi public records that sometimes take extra effort to produce.

b. *Consistency with Previous Disclosures*

The SBM investigator will not only look at all the information in the APH, but also what was previously disclosed on other applications such as law school applications, undergrad applications, job applications, etc. Failure to disclose or provide updates to these applications can be a serious issue for the investigators and the Standing Committee even if later disclosed on the APH. It is important to correct any inconsistencies if you know about them prior to submitting your APH.

5. Financial Disclosures

In terms of personal finances, the applicant should examine his or her credit score and all checking accounts to determine if there was ever a bounced check. Frequently, lay people consider overdrafts covered by the bank to not be returned, or bounced, checks, even though an overdraft indicates money was drawn from an account in which there were insufficient funds. Other consequences such as bankruptcy and defaulting on multiple creditors must also be fully disclosed.

As the cost of law school increases and some applicants have been adversely affected by the real estate and job markets, the District and Standing Committees are sensitive to the financial hardships suffered by some applicants. The issue becomes more acute when the applicant's finances evidence irresponsibility or disregard for creditors. Again, do not try to soft pedal the reasons for financial problems. It creates more issues to be scrutinized when the applicant tries to explain and this new explanation becomes a statement of the applicant's character that can be misinterpreted.

The bottom line with financial disclosures is simple: attorneys deal with other people's money in one way or another. Imprudence with one's personal finances can be interpreted as a problem for the paying public who hires attorneys.

6. Litigation History

Some applicants come from industries or businesses that expose them to multiple lawsuits such as landlords, collection agencies and so forth. Some applicants have multiple ownerships in companies that have lengthy litigation histories. As far as SBM is concerned, all applicants must disclose their litigation history. The applicant should anticipate this when beginning the application and completing these requirements. Sources for help include PACER (for federal court cases), state and local computer systems for circuit and local cases and other common databases available through credit agencies and private investigators.

7. Employment History

Applicants are required to disclose their employment history including internships and volunteer work. Your employment records may be scrutinized if a dismissal was reported. Which records actually appear during a background check are an entirely different matter.

All applicants must sign a general release included in the APH Application. The SBM investigator will seek employment records where the applicant admits being fired or dismissed. There are a number of federal and state laws governing employment records. Individual employers have their own policies regarding what records are retained, disclosed, or destroyed. Out of fear of litigation or lack of concern, not all employment records will be produced. A disclosure about an adverse employment action will generate a request for the records that may not always be honored.

Applicants are advised to assume otherwise and be prepared for pertinent records to be released. The investigator will follow up on letters, statements, etc. to clarify whatever facts are available. The applicant needs to make proper disclosure on the APH to ensure maintaining a high level of integrity in presenting all the facts.

THE GOAL

The goal of the application process is to vet an applicant for the protection of the public and maintain the integrity of the law profession. By being thorough and complete, an applicant expedites the process and allows the State Bar to have a complete picture of who the applicant is. For many, this will not be a problem. They have not had the contacts in business, problems with finances, criminal contacts, lawsuits, security clearances or other problems that may be a poor reflection on one's character. Just the same, any minor contacts must be disclosed as readily as other mundane matters. Careless applicants are always surprised how often a simple problem is made more complex by the failure to disclose.

SUMMARY

- Carefully complete the Affidavit of Personal History
- Err on the side of over-disclosure
- Ask for help from SBM or other sources if you need it
- If you anticipate a problem, consult with counsel prior to submitting your APH

Chapter Three

THE DISTRICT COMMITTEE AND THE DISTRICT COMMITTEE MEETING

One has a greater sense of
degradation after an interview
with a doctor than from any
human experience.
-Alice Jones

It ain't the heat, it's the
humility.
-Lawrence Peter Berra

Chapter Three

The District Committee

The State Bar of Michigan requires all applicants to meet all of the requirements of membership before a license will be issued. The first requirement is that the applicant graduate from an ABA approved law school. The second requirement is that the applicant takes and passes the MPRE with a score of 85 or higher. The third requirement is that the applicant successfully passes the Michigan Bar Examination with a combined score of 135 or higher. Finally, the applicant must demonstrate "good character and fitness" to the State Bar by submitting an Affidavit of Personal History (APH) to SBM for a background investigation and review.

As noted in Chapter 2, this process is generally not a problem for most applicants especially if there is no adverse conduct in their history or other facts that would bring issues regarding character and fitness into question. Even with perceived negative past conduct, it will not necessarily delay the application if the conduct is properly and fully disclosed. If this is the case, the applicant should not have any problem demonstrating his or her current requisite good character and fitness.

The APH review and investigation, while seemingly eternal in the minds of most applicants, is a routine part of the process. This is the case if there are no adverse facts in the applicant's history that would warrant further investigation and all sources, references, addresses, prior employers, schools and similar information are verified as true and accurate.

Some applicants have a little more to explain. It could be something as simple as an extensive litigation background (i.e. landlords), a financial problem (i.e. bankruptcy as result of medical bills or other personal tragedy) or a criminal incident at some point in the applicant's past, including a juvenile history. While these items alone may require further scrutiny by the investigators, they would not necessarily require a District Committee hearing. Once explained, the application process would continue and a favorable report may follow.

Notice of District Committee Meeting

However, when there is a question that cannot be satisfied with a simple letter of explanation or the investigator(s) feel there are too many questions to be asked, the next step in the process begins. It will start with a letter to the applicant from the State Bar Character and Fitness Department informing the applicant that their local District Committee would like to meet with them to discuss certain issues regarding the application to practice law. The issues are specified in the letter and should be of no surprise to the applicant. According to the letter, the meeting is an "informal" meeting where a frank discussion will ensue to talk about the application and the issues surrounding it. Examples of such letters are found in Appendix D.

An "Informal" Meeting

The District Committee meeting with an applicant is dictated by the State Bar of Michigan Standing Committee on Character and Fitness Rules of Procedure. Specifically, Rule B dictates the duties and responsibilities of the District Committee (See Appendix A).

Let us look a little closer at this process. First, the title "informal meeting" is not entirely accurate. This meeting definitely has a more formal atmosphere. It usually takes place at a courthouse or in the law offices of one of the District Committee Members. Everyone will be wearing business attire. The District Committee Members have been provided with a full copy of the applicant's APH and the SBM file derived from the investigation. The committee members will discuss why the issues identified by the investigators could prevent the applicant from practicing law. Although this meeting is "informal," given the potential outcomes, it should not be taken lightly.

What makes it an informal meeting is that the State Bar of Michigan is not represented by counsel and there is no formal record made of the proceedings. No individual gives sworn testimony and there is not a single format for the District Panel to follow other than rules set forth by the Standing Committee on Character and Fitness (see Appendix A). While the meeting is recorded, the recording is not transcribed.[8] There is no set structure for the meeting beyond the formalities set forth at the beginning and end of the meeting. Sometimes it starts with questions or the panel asks the applicant for a narrative. Panelists are typically well prepared but sometimes they prepare closer to the hearing date. The panel members are all volunteers so work and scheduling pressures can put them at a disadvantage in being fully prepared for the District meeting. Thus, the burden of knowledge and preparation rests squarely on the applicant.

The District Committee

District Committees are made up of volunteer attorneys who practice within the geographic boundaries of the District who are invited to join the committee by the District Chairman. Each District reflects the same geographical divisions of the State Bar of Michigan. It is a professional distinction to be invited to join the Committee. There are several committee members each with varying experience. The committee members serve two terms and may also serve on the Standing Committee.

The attorneys on this committee are both concerned with applicants who wish to join the bar and sympathetic to their feelings at the time of the interview. Senior members of the Committee have extensive experience interviewing applicants and have a firm understanding of the standard for applicants to meet. Junior members are both concerned with the applicant and treating him or her fairly given their own experience. They also bring their individual experience and personal prejudices to each meeting. All members of the committee deserve respect for their willingness to participate as well as the feedback they frequently provide to applicants.

---

[8]   The tape recording made during the meeting is for the exclusive use of the District Committee, the Standing Committee and SBM with few exceptions.

It may be difficult for applicants who have had a negative experience before the District Committee or perceived the Committee's conduct to be adversarial to not take this treatment personally. These situations manifest in a few different ways:

1. 1) **You're correct** – a panelist really has a problem with something you have done, how you explained it or what you have done or not done subsequently. In short, there is not much you can do about that state of affairs except to be honest about the issue and answer the panel's questions.

2. 2) **Their questions were adversarial** – This committee is made up of attorneys; it is natural that any questions regarding your credentials will be asked in adversarial manner. If you are the sensitive type, it will feel this way no matter what. You will want to desensitize yourself to hearing this criticism because it will come up more than you would like.

3. 3) **You're not objective about the experience** – When you are under verbal assault during your interview, you do not always perceive the situation correctly. Subtleties in questions, softball follow-up questions and the body language of the panel are all things lost on the applicant who is upset or not prepared. Listen carefully to the questions and hear what is being asked.

4. 4) **A combination of the above factors**—It can be a jarring experience to be called out in the manner only a District Committee can do. What is most important about any of these feelings or emotions is to maintain your composure and display good manners no matter how you feel on the inside.

The Interview

Once the formalities of the meeting are met, the interview commences. Without a formal structure, a discussion surrounding the applicant and the issues begins. It can last for a half hour or a half day. The standard for the applicant is to demonstrate that he or she currently possesses the requisite character and fitness by clear and convincing evidence.

Some applicants bring letters of recommendation, medical records, and treatment letters from therapists to support their statements at the meeting. These will be received by the District panel though may not be fully considered or understood at the time of receipt. (Note that any records presented at the District Committee meeting that have not yet been given to the State Bar should also be provided to SBM as soon as possible).

This interview has ramifications for any future contact with the State Bar of Michigan. After the meeting, an opinion is drafted by the Committee reflecting its findings and view in a recommendation regarding the applicant's presentation that day. Thus, if the applicant is unprepared or unaware of the full extent of the investigation, they will be operating in the dark. More likely, if they were unsure how the State Bar felt prior to the District Committee meeting, many applicants learn quickly how their character is being questioned.

At the interview, three or more attorneys who have reviewed the application package and considered carefully what the applicant has said will be in attendance. Given the importance of the result, it is neither the place for off-the-cuff comments nor inappropriate humor. There are several different people in the room who will perceive what the applicant says in many ways. They come from different legal disciplines and may find reasons to disagree with the applicant based on their personal experience or possible personal predisposition. Because the Committee is exclusively comprised of licensed Michigan attorneys, the applicant will sometimes find adversarial undertones during the proceeding. What the applicant thought would be an informal discussion seems more like an inquisition.

The District Committee Decision and its Aftermath

After the interview, the Committee will discuss the results and each member's thoughts regarding the applicant's presentation and the facts at issue. The Committee can recommend unanimous approve of the applicant's character and fitness or issue a split recommendation. The Committee could find the applicant does not possess the requisite character and fitness to practice unanimously or by split opinion. Those recommendations are all delivered to the Standing Committee and are concurrently communicated to the applicant.

Some panels will go into a brief executive session to see if consensus can be reached and a verbal opinion may be given to the applicant on that day. Some panels do not go into executive session, even with positive findings. It is the choice of the panel chair.

If the Committee believes the applicant is unprepared or still suffers from the disability for the conduct that brings the applicant before it, the Committee will not make a favorable recommendation to the Standing Committee. If that is the case, the applicant will then be compelled to either withdraw their application or appear before the Standing Committee for a hearing.

Sometimes, the panel will delay its decision in order to give the applicant time to present additional evidence to support his or her position. These requests should be handled expeditiously and as the panel chair requests.

The rules provide that the District Committee recommendation must be submitted to SBM within 30 days after the hearing. However, that is a soft deadline and can take longer depending on the complexity of the opinion, the working schedule of the panelist writing the opinion, etc.

STANDARD OF REVIEW

The District Committee references the Standing Committee on Character and Fitness Rules E3 and E4 in formulating its review of the behavior of the applicant in question (See Appendix A).

Behaviors addressed by the District Committee

Rule E3 addresses the issues of behavior that would bring one before the District Committee for a hearing. This would include unlawful conduct, academic misconduct, making a false statement, misconduct in employment and any other acts of dishonesty, fraud, deceit or misrepresentation.

Other issues that come before the District Committee include neglect of financial responsibilities or professional obligations, abuse of legal process, violation of a court order, evidence of mental or emotional instability and evidence of drug or alcohol dependency.

Finally, denial of admission to another state bar, practicing law without a license and other disciplinary actions issued by other professional agencies may be considered by the District Committee. All of the foregoing activities are grounds for the District Committee to make a recommendation against admission.

<u>Mitigating Factors</u>

Rule E4 deals with the factors that the District Committee can consider in light of any allegations regarding conduct discussed in Rule E3. These mitigating factors would include the applicant's age at the time of the conduct, how long it has been since the conduct occurred, the seriousness of the conduct and the reliability of the information concerning the conduct and repeated behavior.

Factors underlying the conduct are also considered. The District Committee will look for the cumulative effect of this conduct in light of the rest of the applicant's application. Evidence of rehabilitation includes positive social contributions since the conduct in question, the applicant's candor in the admissions process, the materiality of such admissions or misrepresentations to the process, affirmative efforts to rectify the situation or prevent future occurrences and the timeliness of cooperation with the application investigation process. These factors are weighed by the District Committee in determining a recommendation.

<u>Standard of Proof</u>

The standard of proof for admission to the practice of law is whether the applicant can prove by clear and convincing evidence that he or she currently possesses the requisite character and fitness to practice law. The burden is on the applicant. The statutory citation for what constitutes the requisite standard is purposely vague and open to interpretation. Rule 15 of the State Bar of Michigan Rules sets forth the procedural rules for applicants to be processed by the State Bar of Michigan for submission to the Board of Law Examiners.

MCL 600.934 sets forth the statutory authority for character and fitness. The statute provides in relevant part:

> 600.934 Qualifications for admission to bar; "good moral character" defined; election to use multi-state bar examination scaled score; disclosure of score.
>
> Sec. 934.
>
> (1) A person is qualified for admission to the bar of this state who proves to the satisfaction of the board of law examiners that he or she is a person of good moral character, is 18 years of age or older, has the required general education, learning in the law, and fitness and ability to enable him or her to practice law in the courts of record of this state, and that he or she intends in good faith to practice or teach law in this state. Additional requirements concerning the qualifications for admission are contained in subsequent sections of this chapter. As used in this subsection, "good moral character" means good moral character as defined and determined under 1974 PA 381, MCL 338.41 to 338.47.[9] Also see http://legislature.mi.gov/doc.aspx?mcl-338-41

The case law supporting this statute has largely left the State Bar of Michigan with broad discretion. It is not fully illustrative regarding the nature of the standard. It is not a black or white

---

[9] MCL 600.934 is discussed in greater detail in Chapter 1 of this volume.

standard but provides the applicant with enough gray area within which to effectively argue his or her case. Although this leaves the applicant with the added challenge of meeting the standard as it is understood by the members of the District Committee, there is room for the applicant to articulate his or her position

The best advice is simple: Be prepared, keep in mind the factors in Rules E4 and address the problem straight on. By doing so, the applicant is showing more character then by trying to explain away, minimize or hide a given issue.

TIPS TO PREPARE FOR YOUR DISTRICT COMMITTEE HEARING

1.<u>Order the complete file from the State Bar.</u> For $20, the applicant will be given not only all of the information they have provided to the State Bar, but all of the information gathered by the investigators. This may include correspondence from employers, previous schools, copies of letters of endorsement from sponsors to the bar, financial records including a credit history, criminal records, court records, divorce records, business records and social security records. This is not an all-inclusive list. With the Internet and availability of information, the State Bar does a very thorough investigation in a relatively short period of time. By having this file, the applicant will know exactly what the District Committee Members have before them and can prepare for the questions they may receive during the "informal meeting."

2.<u>Be prepared to give full and open answers regarding any seemingly adverse information.</u> One of the hardest things we do as human beings is admitting our faults. No one wants to look bad or be perceived as a bad person. However, in order to successfully navigate a District Committee panel, the applicant must be unequivocal and clear in the answers s/he provides, regardless of how bad the behavior seems or how poorly the applicant feels it reflects on his or her character. If the applicant cannot discuss these matters openly with the panel, the applicant can almost be certain he or she will not receive a favorable recommendation.

Most applicants who are delayed in their application are delayed because they fail to fully disclose past transgressions or they shade the facts of such transgressions in order to protect their self-image. This is the greatest mistake an applicant can make. For instance, if the applicant is uncertain about their conduct after a criminal arrest, they should be sure to read the police report and their answer on the APH and be prepared to explain any discrepancies between the two. Better yet, make sure the answer presented to the State Bar acknowledges the applicant's version as well as the police version of the event, if they differ. An interesting phenomenon recently observed is when applicants have actually made clear disclosures on their answers, but then cannot discuss the information in person. If the applicant has that problem or thinks they do, it is very important they get use to discussing these difficult facts with others. Consider practicing with an attorney or trusted friend until you feel more comfortable.

3.<u>Consider Hiring Counsel.</u> Why should an applicant want to bring an attorney to an "informal meeting?" The answer is because there is a lot at stake. This is a perfect time not to let your ego get the better of you. If the matter is not handled properly, your application can be delayed for a year or more. A worst case scenario can be that the applicant's appearance before the District Committee could lead to more issues being presented to the Standing Committee. In a worst-case scenario, the applicant could receive an adverse recommendation; does not challenge it, and has to wait two years before he or she can reapply. By bringing an attorney who understands the application process to the meeting, the applicant will not be traversing this challenging path alone and has a professional advocate assisting to establish why s/he possesses good character and fitness. An attorney who is familiar with the proceedings can properly prepare the applicant for the questions they will face, the answers they will present in response and the tenor of the response. Applicants who enter the meeting with an attorney are not thought to be "guilty" but rather treated with respect and deference because of the role that their advocate will be expected to play in the process. This is not to imply however, that applicants who choose to forego counsel are treated with any less respect of deference.

Experienced advocates will not only know members of the Committee, but will be familiar with some of the personal characteristics they bring to the hearing. A good advocate cannot only help the applicant prepare for the hearing, but help to assert dispositive and exculpatory facts which can make the difference between a favorable recommendation and an unfavorable recommendation.

Unfortunately, applicants who are more likely to be called before a District Committee will not always have the opportunity to prepare for it while in law school. Most law schools discuss the application process at the onset of law school and then commence to usually focus more on the present day education they provide. Although law schools do review the application process, its importance seems to be lost on or ignored by many of the applicants. It is the responsibility of the applicant to learn about the process and how it relates to them. To not give due attention of the relevance of all aspects of an applicant's presentation to their future licensing board defeats the process. It is even advised to review the application process before application to law school. This way, any potential applicant is aware of the expectations and the potential issues he or she will have to address and make the determination whether law school is the proper career path. A license to practice law is not an entitlement, regardless of the hours spent studying, the money spent the commitment of time.

As soon as a law student is enrolled, it is important to look to the future by contemplating any circumstances that may raise questions in a future investigation. It would be wise to look at the questions in the State Bar of Michigan application and see what your answers would be. This foresight will allow the applicant to anticipate issues, mitigate where necessary and lessen tension in confronting possible shame and humiliation that may arise.

SUMMARY

Be prepared to discuss your issue(s) and make sure the panel understands all the facts, not just the negative ones.

1. Remember the standard to meet: Clear and convincing evidence of the requisite good moral character and fitness to practice law.
2. Know your APH and review the SBM file before the meeting takes place.
3. Ask for help if you need it or think you may need it.
4. Be yourself.

Chapter Four

THE STANDING COMMITTEE AND STANDING COMMITTEE HEARING

Character cannot be developed
in ease and quiet. Only
through experience of trial
and suffering can the soul be
strengthened, ambition
inspired, and success achieved.
-Helen Keller

Adversity is the trial of
principle. Without it a man
hardly knows whether he is
honest or not.
-Henry Fielding

Chapter Four

The Standing Committee

The State Bar of Michigan handles the application process. After the applicant files an application, it is reviewed by investigators who make recommendations whether further information is needed from them or not. Sometimes this takes the form of an inquiry letter and other times it requires more extensive information from the applicant. As discussed in Chapter 3, many times, the applicant will be called before a District Committee that is made up of local attorneys who volunteer their time to review the applicant's documentation and make a determination whether there exists any reason to question the applicant's character and fitness. More likely than not, applicants who appear before the District Committee are generally given a positive recommendation and then approved by the Standing Committee on Character and Fitness and ultimately the Board of Law Examiners.

However, not all applicants who appear before the District Committee are finished with the application process. The findings and report of the District Committee are not binding on the Standing Committee but are given serious consideration. Depending upon the recommendation given by the District Committee, the Standing Committee may deem the application requires further review and, thus, the more formal hearing before it is necessary.[10]

Applicants who appear before the Standing Committee have already been to the District Committee hearing. For whatever reason, the applicant has not convinced the Standing Committee of his or her good character and fitness despite the fact the applicant may have received a positive recommendation from the District Committee. Even with a positive recommendation from District Committee, the applicant still may be called before the Standing Committee for a formal hearing.

TRIAL EXPERIENCE

The Standing Committee hearing is essentially an administrative law trial. It is governed by the State Bar of Michigan Standing Committee on Character and Fitness Rules of Procedure (See Appendix D). The State Bar will appoint an attorney to represent its interest and the Standing Committee is made up of up to five attorneys experienced in the matters of character and fitness applications. They consider the issues presented by the State Bar that may draw the application into question and then render a recommendation whether the applicant possesses the requisite character and fitness to practice. If additional issues arise upon review of the State Bar Counsel, additional issues may be added to the hearing. The burden of proving character and fitness lies with the applicant.

---

[10] Rule B.9. SBM Standing Committee on Character and Fitness Rules of Procedure

The applicant may represent him or herself or may hire counsel. It is advisable that the applicant hire counsel, lest their ego get the better of them.

Matters come before the Standing Committee after the District Committee has rendered its recommendation. The District Committee recommendation will be considered by the Standing Committee who will then indicate whether further inquiry is required. If it is, a notice is sent to the applicant explaining what issues will be explored at the hearing. At this point, the Standing Committee is generally agreeing with the District Committee's recommendation that an applicant lacks the requisite character or is disagreeing with a finding of an applicant's character. If it perceives the applicant lacks character, the applicant must request the hearing within 10 days. Otherwise, the applicant's file will be closed and he or she must wait two years to re-apply.

If the applicant has a positive recommendation from the District Committee, the Standing Committee hearing is still required. However, the applicant will be going into the hearing on more positive footing. The applicant still must participate in the process.

Prehearing Conference

Prior to the hearing, a pre-hearing telephone conference is held to determine evidentiary issues, witness lists and other housekeeping matters. Questions about whether a five member committee will be waived (to a three member panel) and whether Regular Members may sit (or allow for Advisory Members to sit on the panel) are determined at that conference. Regular Members are experienced members of the Standing Committee. Panel chairs are always Regular Members. Advisory Members are generally newer members of the Standing Committee but some of them have many years experience as an Advisor. They usually have prior experience as District Committee Members but not always. These conferences are generally conducted by telephone with a formal order published to all parties following the call. Although it is an administrative law type of proceeding, the Committee does not strictly follow Michigan's Rules of Evidence or Civil Procedure nor it is bound to do so. Rather, it seeks guidance from those rules in conducting a hearing. State Bar Counsel is also drawn from the Standing Committee.

Exhibits

Prior to the hearing, the State Bar publishes all of the exhibits in a bound book, whose cover only identifies the applicant by their application number. Prior to the hearing, the applicant or State Bar can question or move to strike exhibits. The applicant may add exhibits and/or adopt exhibits proposed by the State Bar. Either party may also publish supplements to the bound book. The witnesses are identified and informal discussions are held between the applicant (and applicant's counsel) and the State Bar Counsel as to the nature and expected testimony of the witnesses to be presented and whether testimony will occur in person or by telephone conference. All exhibits must be submitted to the SBM within 30 days of the hearing to ensure they are published in time for the panelists to review prior to the hearing.

The notices of hearing are part of the bound book as is the recommendation of the District Committee. Relevant records from the Affidavit of Personal History (APH) are also cited. They are given exhibit numbers that are used as reference during the hearing. The Applicant's exhibits are also listed as long as the State Bar receives them in a timely manner.

If other records are produced beyond the cutoff date for the bound book, they may be introduced at the discretion of the Standing Committee Chairperson and/or with consent of the State Bar counsel. The disadvantage of producing records beyond the cutoff date is that the panelists may not have an opportunity to review them prior to the hearing.

Scheduling the Hearing

The hearing itself will be scheduled according to the collective schedules of all counsel, the committee members and the applicant. This generally requires six to eight weeks at a minimum to schedule hearings. Sometimes the scheduling is extended in time based upon the individual needs of the applicant. Examples of such delays may involve the completion of rehabilitative activities such as an LJAP (Lawyers and Judges Assistance Program) contract or closing out a criminal probation file. This timing is unique to each applicant.

A WORD ABOUT THE STANDARD OF PROOF

The applicant bears the burden to prove that he or she currently possesses the current character and fitness to practice law. The standard of proof is clear and convincing evidence.[11] This lies somewhere between evidence beyond a reasonable doubt and a preponderance of the evidence. In rough mathematical terms it is between 65% and 75% certainty regarding a given issue. There is no way to say whether the applicant's testimony and documents are sufficient to meet the standard. It tends to be more of a standard that meets the eye of the beholder (i.e. the panelists making a determination on character and fitness) and the collective wisdom of the panel. Thus, it is important to understand this audience as best as you can.

THE HEARING

The hearing can take place in a number of different places. This would include a private law office, a courthouse or at the State Bar of Michigan building in Lansing. Depending upon the size of the room, it can be quite an intimate experience (as well as an intimidating one). The Committee Members will be in the room along with State Bar Counsel, a representative from the State Bar (one of the investigators or the manager of Character and Fitness), a court reporter, the applicant and/or applicant's counsel.

Introduction and Opening

The hearing begins with an introduction of all participants for the record. Once the introductions have been made, the formal rules are reviewed and the applicant confirms that the quorum is present and responds to the question whether there have been any changes to the application since it had been submitted. Usually, application changes are made in writing. However, if there are last minute changes to be made that day, those should be put on the record and then later submitted in writing to the State Bar and the Committee.

---

[11]   Rule D.3. SBM Standing Committee on Character and Fitness Rules of Procedure

The proceeding then allows for opening statements to be made by State Bar Counsel and/or the applicant's counsel or the applicant. Opening statements are optional and can be waived. Since the applicant has the burden of proof, the applicant presents his or her case first.

Applicant/Witness Presentation

Applicant's Testimony

Because the hearing is about the applicant, the panel is usually focused on hearing from the applicant. The Committee prefers to hear from the applicant first and then from the applicant's witnesses. This schedule of testimony is not always possible due to scheduling conflicts of the witnesses. Just the same, it is encouraged that the applicant should present first from a tactical standpoint. Ideally, the applicant should be the best witness and you want to make your presentation strong from the beginning.

Testimony is weighted in a number of different ways. The applicant's testimony means the most to the outcome. The panel is assessing current character and fitness from the applicant. Body language, speech characteristics, quirks and other manifestations of anxiety are understood and expected. The qualities all applicants need to bring to their testimony are openness and sincerity.

Supporting Witness Testimony

Other witnesses being offered should be relevant and give support to the central position of the applicant. The quality of the witnesses, the position they have had to observe the applicant, their knowledge of the standard of fitness and other factors such as possible prejudices will all be considered. The witnesses for the applicant may testify as to their knowledge of the applicant, circumstances surrounding issues before the Committee and related issues. It is important to keep these witnesses focused on the central issue of the applicant's character. Once they have testified, State Bar counsel has an opportunity to cross examine the witness as well as the Committee members. You will always have the opportunity to redirect.

The most important element for any witness will be the quality of his or her testimony. For example, attorneys tend to be good witnesses to call in these hearings as they are tacitly assumed to know the standard of practice and also, by testifying on behalf of the applicant, give their implicit or explicit character and fitness approval of the applicant. Spouses, family members and friends sometimes can provide insight to the panel in regard to issues that come before it. However, these witnesses can sometimes wear their prejudice on their sleeve and can lessen the overall effectiveness of the testimony. Colleagues from the workplace and educators can also provide insights. The requirement for calling any of these witnesses would be the nature of their knowledge of the applicant's character and their ability to advance the proposition that the applicant possess current requisite character and fitness.

Documents and Exhibits

Any documents the applicant chooses to include should be admissible under the rules of evidence. If the applicant needs to lay a foundation for those documents, it would be important to do so well before the hearing and, hopefully, with the stipulation of the State Bar Counsel. While it happens infrequently, sometimes matters do become contentious and evidentiary issues become the focus of the hearing rather than the character and fitness of the applicant.

<u>State Bar Presentation</u>

The State Bar may also call witnesses on its behalf. Although this does not happen as frequently as the applicant calling witnesses, in some situations it is relevant for the State Bar to bring witnesses (such as former employers, victims in criminal situations, medical treaters who may have found mental instability, etc.). Generally speaking, the applicant will know the nature of the testimony to be offered. Just the same, it is important for counsel to make sure that he or she understands the nature of any witnesses' testimony. In extraordinary circumstances, pre-hearing depositions can be taken with the consent of the chair and opposing counsel. The chair can also subpoena witnesses.

<u>Rebuttal</u>

As the applicant bears the burden in the matter, the applicant also has the ability to rebut the State Bar witnesses. This is not frequently seen in most hearings due to the open nature of the discovery process. Sometimes, the committee will reopen proofs to clarify an issue. It usually will be evident which issue is unclear and why further testimony is sought. It is difficult to say whether this is good or bad. It does indicate that there is some clarification sought by the Committee. The applicant and his or her counsel need to pay close attention to these proceedings as they present both opportunities and hazards.

<u>Closing</u>

At the end of the hearing, the applicant and State Bar Counsel have the ability to offer closing remarks. The applicant can also rebut the State Bar Counsel's closing. Once the proofs and the closing statements have been made, the matter is then submitted to the Committee Members for their consideration.

THE WITNESSES

<u>Presentation and Preparation</u>

Both the State Bar and applicant have the right to present witnesses at a Standing Committee Hearing. Generally, witnesses are listed in the Proposed Prehearing Order, although if another witness becomes relevant to the matter, that order can be amended. Because the court rules are a matter of guidance and not of direct ruling, there is no true scheduling order to be enforced. Thus, it is possible to have a "surprise" witness. In practice, most counsel show each other common professional courtesy in regard to additional witnesses by giving some notification ahead of time. All the proofs being offered outside of the rules are admissible at the discretion of the Committee Chair whose decision is final.

Preparation of the Applicant

The main witness is the applicant. Like any other hearing or trial, the applicant must be thoroughly prepared with the knowledge of the issues to be examined and for extensive cross-examination. The best service an applicant can do for him or herself is to thoroughly consider what questions will be offered in cross-examination and be prepared to discuss them at length.

Beyond thorough preparation, the applicant must truly know him or herself. When you first meet clients, they may have a difficult time discussing the issues that have delayed their application. Management and understanding of these matters is key to the applicant's success; whatever measures are necessary to heighten the self-awareness of the applicant ought to be utilized.

Preparation of Character Witnesses

Because the applicant is the person of interest to the Standing Committee, other witnesses need to be offered sparingly and with a relevant and definite purpose. It is not unusual to have persons who want to testify on behalf of an applicant appear at the hearing without being thoroughly prepared for possible questions about the applicant. These types of "surprises" should be avoided as they sometimes lead to uncomfortable testimony by the character witness. Examples of unpreparedness are when a witness is asked a question about a particular incident for which he or she lacks any knowledge and then when asked a follow-up question whether that knowledge would change their opinion of the applicant's character, leads to a negative recommendation for the applicant. Thus, thorough preparation of supporting witnesses (e.g. full prior disclosure by applicant to witness) is just as important as that of the applicant. Make sure these witnesses are prepared ahead of time and are provided with some written indication of the issues concerning the applicant.

Medical Professional Witnesses

Other relevant witnesses who may testify would be professionals (i.e. doctors, alcohol counselors or therapists) from whom the applicant has sought treatment. The most important thing any witness will have will be insight regarding the applicant and to the stated issues. Sheer volume and number of witnesses alone is rarely helpful and sometimes can actually be harmful to the applicant's case.

Some professional witnesses are reticent to testify because of poor experiences they have had in court proceedings. First, it is important that you distinguish this particular hearing from a court hearing. Unlike a trial court where the professional witness will appear in front of a jury on the open record, this hearing is confidential with a sealed record. The witness's testimony during this hearing is considered a confidential part of the State Bar application process and thus, does not become public knowledge. See the article set forth in Appendix H for a professional counselor's view of the application process and sample questions in Appendix F.

Second, professionals should know that the inquiries from the panel will be more focused on the applicant than on any of the witness' qualifications. While professional qualifications are important, how the professional has interacted with the applicant and to what extent it is relevant to the issue of character is more important.

Third, the professional witnesses' records are frequently considered to be relevant to the proceedings. Thus, before offering a professional witness, his or her records should be presented either in a summary and an unedited form. It would be helpful to the panel to have those records in the bound book so they are more familiar with the intervention and efforts of the witness. Ideally, the unedited record would come prepared with a summary. This is helpful for many members of the Standing Committee who prefer to rely on the testimony and guidance of the summary rather than coming to their own interpretation of unedited or handwritten medical or other records. The applicant should make sure his or her testimony is consistent with those records or, if it is going to be inconsistent, be prepared to testify and explain the inconsistency. Likewise, the professional witness needs to be thoroughly prepared and any inconsistency from the case of the applicant needs to be properly vetted by counsel in order to achieve the best insights.

Legal Professionals as Witnesses

The testimony of attorneys and judges can be very helpful to an applicant. As licensed attorneys and judges are part of the State Bar, their opinions tend to carry more weight. It is presumed that the attorney or judge has a better understanding of the standard of conduct and would bring the same into the hearing. After all, any attorney or judge who testifies on behalf of an applicant knows in his or her mind that the applicant could very well be a colleague or adversary with whom they will have to conduct business in the future.

As a practical matter, not every attorney or judge is as articulate of their understanding of the standard for admission as the preceding paragraph would presume. An applicant or applicant's counsel should be mindful to ask questions of an attorney or judge witness to make sure that they not only understand the standard, but that they can also readily articulate why the applicant meets that standard. Like any other witnesses, the experiences and insights an attorney or judge witness could offer need to be drawn out, but the focus of the questions should be mostly about insights that could be offered regarding the applicant. This proceeding is not the appropriate place for a legal witness to expound at length on their credentials in an effort to somehow bolster the credentials of the applicant. See Appendix E for sample questions.

Other Potential Witnesses

Lay witnesses may also be helpful regarding a particular issue. Members of the applicant's Alcoholics Anonymous group, co-workers who are not in the legal profession and family members who can lend a particular insight may also be helpful to the process. Like any other witnesses, they need to be educated regarding the standard at hand and prepared in answering questions in a manner that helps the applicant. See Appendix G for sample questions.

It is safe to say that most applicants have a circle of family and friends who will support them no matter what the issue may be. These individuals are not always appropriate, but can be helpful in certain situations. Their support is important to the applicant outside of the hearing process, but probably will not assist in clarifying the issues for the Standing Committee.

An overriding concern for any applicant is the length of time you have a witness testify. Lengthy testimony does not encourage positive results unless that testimony is relevant and tied specifically to all of the issues at hand. Many Standing Committee members who conduct the hearings are generally of the mindset that the faster the applicant can get to the point of the witnesses' testimony, the better off it will go. Nobody wants to hear long-winded witnesses who are not testifying directly to the issue at hand.

I suggest that all questions for direct examination be prepared ahead of time by counsel and provided to the witnesses to practice to the point that he or she is comfortable in answering the questions. If a witness provides any surprises or revelations during testimony, the questioning can be adjusted to work around them or to address the potentially adverse answers.

DECISION

Some Committees will go into an executive session, with the other parties excluded from the room. During this session, the Committee Members will discuss the testimony, evidence and impressions about the applicant's case and attempt to come to a consensus. If the Committee is able to come to a consensus it will usually let the applicant know that day. If the Committee is unable to come to a consensus, then it may continue its deliberations at a later date after considering the hearing transcript, other documents or reschedule the matter for further proceedings.

If the decision is clear-cut, the applicant is generally told the same day as the hearing. One of the members of the Committee is then assigned the task of writing the recommendation that is then circulated and approved. Once it has been approved by all Committee Members, the recommendation is then transmitted along with the entire application file to the Board of Law Examiners (BLE) for its review.

BLE Review and Decision

The Board of Law Examiners has the final say in the matter. The Board is the official state agency that issues the license. The Board may accept the positive recommendation of the Committee, not approve it or ask for more information from the applicant. Likewise, the Board may do the same thing with a negative recommendation from the Standing Committee. If the Board chooses to have the applicant appear for further proceedings, it is considered a de novo hearing with the reintroduction of proofs and reliance on the record made at the Standing Committee hearing. The nature and timing of such hearings is the subject of Chapter Five.

CONCLUSION

The Standing Committee hearing is critically important for any applicant whose character and fitness is at issue. The price of not being fully prepared is high. Not only does the applicant have to wait two years or longer to reapply in the State of Michigan, he or she may be precluded from successfully applying to other states by the very fact they were denied by Michigan. That would almost certainly raise concerns with other jurisdictions who might consider the Michigan application and its ramifications about the applicant's character in its character and fitness process.

Success at this hearing means receiving a positive recommendation from the Standing Committee. It does not mean the applicant lived a perfect life and cannot guarantee everything they do in the future will be perfect. However, a positive recommendation is based upon the applicant meeting his/her burden of proof and has show by clear and convincing evidence that he or she possesses the requisite character and fitness to be admitted to practice law in the State of Michigan.

The choice of an applicant to hire counsel is a personal one. However, with so much at risk, I believe it is imperative to hire counsel so the applicant can make the best case possible without having to rely solely on his or her own resources. Even if the applicant was successful at the District Committee hearing, the formal nature of the Standing Committee hearing demands a higher degree of preparation and objectivity which may be difficult to muster on one's own.

SUMMARY

Your application to become an attorney needs to be a priority. Be truthful. When you find yourself in the hearing stage of the Character and Fitness process, strongly consider obtaining the assistance of counsel.

1. Because the applicant has the burden, it is easier to set the pace and tone of the hearing.
2. Focus your presentation on the applicant and the stated issues. The applicant's testimony and the testimony of supporting witnesses needs to be focused on the issues at hand.
3. Prepare and rehearse your presentation.
4. Know your record well.

Chapter Five

HEARINGS BEFORE THE BOARD OF LAW EXAMINERS

Make sure you have finished
speaking before your audience
has finished listening.
-Dorothy Sarnoff

A man is not finished when
he's defeated he's finished
when he quits.
-Richard Nixon

Chapter Five

Hearings Before Board of Law Examiners

OVERVIEW

A hearing before the Board of Law Examiners may be required or is permitted after the results of the Standing Committee Hearing have been published. The court rules provide for a hearing before the Board of Law Examiners if the Standing Committee's recommendation is not accepted by the Board.[12]

When the Standing Committee makes a recommendation regarding the character and fitness of an applicant, the Board of Law Examiners is free to reject those findings, accept the findings or perform its own inquiry. Such an inquiry would be made in the form of a de novo hearing held in Lansing when the Board sits for its meetings.

By the time the Board of Law Examiners hears the matter, it has the entire investigation file of the applicant from the State Bar of Michigan, the recommendation of the District Committee, and the transcript, evidence and the written recommendation from the Standing Committee.

If the applicant is aggrieved by a negative recommendation from the Standing Committee, the applicant is entitled to have a de novo hearing. If the Standing Committee makes a positive recommendation and the Board of Law Examiners either rejects that recommendation or defers its decision, the applicant is also entitled to a hearing.[13]

<u>Preliminary Matters to the Hearing</u>

Notice of the Board of Law Examiners' final decision will be sent to the applicant after it has been published and approved. The applicant then has sixty days to accept the decision of the Board or to request a hearing. If a hearing is requested, all the applicant's materials generated up to the present date will be bound in books for the hearing and will be provided to all BLE members who will be participating in that meeting. They are similar to the bound books used by the Standing Committee.

Scheduling of these hearings is a little more challenging because of their infrequent nature. The Board of Law Examiners meets every six to eight weeks. Sometimes this is done by telephone. Other times, the BLE members will actually gather in Lansing for a meeting. In order to conduct a hearing, a quorum of the Board of Law Examiners must be present in order to vote. The first available date

---

[12]   Rules for The Board of Law Examiners, Rule 2(C)-2

[13]   *Ibid.*, Rule 2(C)-2

may be three months or more away. It is advisable to accept the first day available if time is of the essence for the applicant.

The State Bar will continue to be represented by the attorney who had previously represented it at the Standing Committee hearing. State Bar Counsel will continue to present the State Bar with issues deemed relevant. Just the same, the burden lies with the applicant to demonstrate that he or she currently possesses the requisite character and fitness by clear and convincing evidence. Through the scheduling process and the decision of the Board of Law Examiners, there is usually a good indication of what issue or issues are problematic for the Board. While the applicant has the right to again present his or her entire case, it is usually better to determine what is at issue for the Board of Law Examiners. This can be done either formally or informally. With this information, the applicant may properly plan the hearing.

The Hearing

One of the strengths of a Board of Law Examiners hearing is that there is already a well-developed record from the Standing Committee hearing. The evidence in that hearing need not be presented again, but should be emphasized in an opening statement or through the testimony of the applicant with the documentary support highlighted either as a separate exhibit to the Board of Law Examiners or as a reference to previously admitted evidence. Witnesses may appear either in person or by telephone. It is important to focus your presentation on the issues that are most vexing to the Board of Law Examiners.

Your audience will be the five members of the Michigan Board of Law Examiners. Their membership is made up of senior attorneys and judges who are appointed by the Michigan Supreme Court and serve 5-year terms. They review all applications that come before the Standing Committee and are familiar with the application process. They have other responsibilities including the preparation and grading of the Michigan Bar Examination.

Procedure

Both sides are entitled to make an opening statement. Since the applicant still has the burden, he or she will present evidence first followed by cross-examination by State Bar Counsel. The members of the Board of Law Examiners may ask questions at any time, including during direct or cross examination of the applicant. Since it is usually the applicant's testimony that is most important, care should be taken in preparing for the testimony to be made before the Board of Law Examiners. Make reference to the previous testimony and transcript as necessary. While it is important to be consistent in the testimony, if any changes come up between the time of the Standing Committee hearing and that of the Board of Law Examiners, take the initiative to bring those changes to the attention of the BLE and acknowledge them. This includes but is not limited to a change in position on an issue, change in life circumstance that affects the issues before the Board of Law Examiners or other important information. Continued counseling would mean that more records would be available to report. Further participation in LJAP or other programming may be supportive.

When the Board of Law Examiners has requested an applicant to appear before it, after the Standing Committee has given its recommendation, make sure to emphasize the testimony that addresses the issues directly. Most likely, the Board of Law Examiners will have specific questions for the applicant. Depending on the tenor of the hearing, the Board may simply start asking questions about their specific concerns.

<u>Preparation of the File</u>

A thorough preparation of the file includes reviewing testimony and evidence, especially testimony from which a decision regarding the applicant's current character and fitness stemmed.

<u>Additional Evidence</u>

If additional documentation exists to support or refute the position of the applicant, it should be addressed at the Board of Law Examiners hearing. It may be included in the bound book of documents, but if it is developed after the time of publication, may be presented live to the members as proposed evidence. Common professional courtesy would call for any documents to be presented to State Bar Counsel and the SBM Investigator as soon as practicable.

<u>Decision and Consequences</u>

Once the proofs have been presented in the hearing, the Board of Law Examiners will usually meet in an executive session and thereafter publish a final decision. This will be sent to the applicant and the SBM. Unlike Standing Committee hearings where the members generally give an indication of how it will rule on the day of the hearing, the Board of Law Examiners tends to publish its decision in the form of a written order after the hearing has been held.

If the Board of Law Examiners has adversely ruled on a matter, the applicant is then barred for two years from the date of the opinion from reapplying to become an attorney.[14] If the Board of Law Examiners' opinion is favorable, then the applicant's credentials to be sworn in as an attorney will be mailed to him or her. The Board of Law Examiners could also decide to defer a matter and allow the applicant to continue the application process after meeting a specific goal (such as finishing a LJAP contract, agreeing to other terms of counseling, paying debt, etc.).

<u>The Last Resort in Michigan State Court</u>

The last resort in this process lies with the Michigan Supreme Court. The court rules provide that an aggrieved applicant may seek a writ of superintendent control with the Michigan Supreme Court. This is a rare occurrence in Michigan. However, it is a provision in the court rules and from time to time, applicants have invoked their rights under these rules in order to pursue their rights by demonstrating for example, that the application was not properly interpreted, there was an abuse of discretion, or that the Standing Committee made a palpable error which prevented them from coming to the proper recommendation to conclude that the applicant possesses the requisite character and fitness.

---

[14]   Rule 2(C)-3 allows the Board to extend the time to wait up to 5 years.

Timothy A. Dinan

Summary

A hearing before the Board of Law Examiners is typically uncommon. It comes on the heels of a Standing Committee hearing or is rooted in the applicant's opinion that he or she has not been given fair treatment in the system. The best preparation for this hearing is to know what issues are most troubling to the Board of Law Examiners. Focus preparation and presentation on those issues. Keep an open mind in regard to potential "creative" solutions that the Board of Law Examiners may be pondering. Think along the lines of what sort of assurances the Board of Law Examiners would want in order for the applicant to be viewed as meeting his or her burden and to receive a law license. Since Michigan does not issue conditional law licenses or grant a probationary period, it is important to identify what problems can be solved through unique and creative solutions. Keep in mind that the goal is to receive a law license, not to rewrite the past.

With these considerations, an applicant can put his or her best foot forward to satisfy the concerns of the Board of Law Examiners.

Chapter Six

FINAL THOUGHTS

Patience, n. A minor form of despair,
disguised as virtue.
-Ambrose Bierce

He that can have patience can
have what he will.
- Benjamin Franklin

Chapter Six

Final Thoughts

Depending on where you are in the process, the thought of going through a lengthy set of hearings in order to obtain your law license can be daunting. If you have never been subject to such intense scrutiny, you will find it to be humiliating and unnerving. The narrow focus on certain aspects of your life seems unfair and skews your idea of who you are. The focus by this process on the negative aspects of your life takes them out of context at times and seems to diminish and cheapen all that you have done to get where you are.

Moreover, it compels you to really look deep inside and reassess everything you have done and want to do. It is difficult to open yourself up to a group of strangers and discuss your private life. It is equally difficult to ask for help from friends, family and other persons in your world. There is so much potential for rejection and disappointment.

<u>Is it Worth the Time?</u>

It takes a long time to be a lawyer. Considering the amount of schooling you have, you may see any further delay as a hindrance. This is understandable. And yes, you may be considering how you are going to pay your loans which will be due or already due.

Most applicants bring a string of successes into this process. For some, this is the first time anyone has ever said 'No' to them. For others, they anticipated this process knowing their path to practice required them to overcome personal and legal challenges. Either way, you are not moving into practice with your cohort. If you passed the bar examination, but haven't cleared C & F, it is awkward to discuss it with your work colleagues and friends.

Lawyers still hold a prestigious role in society. Despite the bad jokes and seemingly endless criticism of lawyers and the law, lawyers have a vital role in helping people navigate the pitfalls and shortcomings of society. Our role as advocates and interpreters of the law cast us as heroes and villains simultaneously. Personalities aside, most lawyers come at the work with respect and understanding for each other. The one time the bar, as a whole, has a chance to screen its membership is through the application process. In Michigan, being selected to the Character and Fitness committee is a privilege and a role each member takes seriously. While they're aware that you are anxiously awaiting your results, they will not be rushed in coming to a conclusion.

The amount of time it takes to complete the character and fitness process is directly related to the number of issues being brought to the panel. In other words, your success is tied entirely to your history and your ability to satisfy the Standing Committee and the Board of Law Examiners that you do not pose a threat to the public or to your fellow lawyers to the integrity and function of the legal system.

The manner in which the investigations and hearings are held is one factor. Since the panels are staffed by volunteers, the time requirements found in the procedures rules are voluntary and there is no method to compel the process to go faster than its volunteers choose to take it.

There are also a number of things that happen behind the scenes. The time it takes to gather records and that numerous investigations are simultaneously taking place also delays your investigation from being completed. Getting records from out of state and updating your application are just some of the examples of delays. If you are delayed in getting records to SBM, it adds time it will take to have those records reviewed and collated into the investigation file.

Is it worth the time? Only you can answer that question. I believe that lawyers who have had to overcome C & F issues or perhaps passed the bar after more than one try tend to value their attorney credentials a bit more than those who did not have to invest more into the process. I believe it is worth the wait. Patience is not only a virtue; it is a necessary survival mechanism.

Time can especially seem to go slow when you are focused on one critical matter, that being your admission to practice. As best as you can, take your focus off of the application process and focus on the other aspects of your life.

What Can I Do to Speed Up the Process ?

The process works best when all deadlines are met, all requests for documents are timely submitted and the information provided is accurate and responsive to the questions. Read the APH directions carefully, be timely in submitting materials and be painstakingly accurate. If you are unclear about a directive, ask for help. Beyond that, I know of no manner of speeding up the necessary work that is done by SBM or the Standing Committee.

When it comes to hearings, there are some procedural steps set forth in Chapter 4 that will secure the necessary volunteers for the process.

How Do I Let My Employers Know About This Process?

In the most direct manner possible. In a word "directly". A number of clients over the years have been hired contingently upon being licensed as an attorney. When this process is delayed, it causes some consternation amongst both employers and employees. Generally speaking, I have found an honest conversation with one's employer is the best approach to dealing with the mystery of when everything will be completed. Employers have needs as well as employees. They recognize the value of a job. However, any job which is premised on a misrepresentation of the facts will not result in a positive long term relationship. In most instances, the employer is willing to wait the appropriate amount of time. I have found that employers frequently sympathize with their employees and prove to be some of the strongest allies when a hearing comes about.

The longer you delay informing your employer, the more uncomfortable the situation will be. If you do lose your job, whether temporarily or permanently, it is better to have that part of the situation addressed or attempt to hold out in vain hopes that you will be able to control the process. It will not happen the way you want it to occur.

Should I Have a Contingency Plan?

Yes. It is always prudent to have a back-up plan as well as a second and even third back-up plan. You may not be able to predict how long it will take for the Committee to complete its work on your application, nor whether you will be successful or not. Even without a license, an individual with a law school education has many marketable skills. They do not need to necessarily relate to the practice of law.

Other Advice:

1.   Keep in mind the fact that this process is ultimately designed to help you get your license. Despite the seemingly draconian rules and lengthy time period it takes, the process is designed to get people through it; most applicants who request a law license and otherwise meet the requirements, become attorneys. Part of the process is the investigation. The other part of the process is introspection for the applicant. It is during this period of time that you learn more about yourself. Take the investigation and its questions to heart; perhaps you will take something away from it besides a license.

2.   If you find out about a health problem like an addiction during the application process, do something about it. The Lawyers Judges Assistance Program (LJAP) is there to help attorneys, judges and law students address their disease. The program addresses many addiction problems confidentially and gets legal professionals the help they need and back to work as soon as it is possible. While not a 'one size fits all suit' it has lots of programming and resources to help

3.   One of the hardest things for most people to do, especially for a young lawyer, is request help. We have been raised in a self-sufficient environment and trained to help others. So when we need help ourselves we tend to be more reluctant to do so. Professional counseling can be a great source of support during the application process and may even establish a base of supportive expert testimony. Make sure whoever you see is aware of the pending application and make sure they are familiarized with the issues bringing you before the Standing Committee. My experience has been positive with counselors and the relationship creates unexpected benefits besides bolstering the strength of your application.

The counseling process can be very valuable not only in the long term, but also in the short term in dealing with the long term implications of practicing law. A good counselor will act as a sounding board for a client and ask the right questions and listen to the answers. It is not unusual for counselors to find other issues and solutions to problems that improve relationships, bring calm and improve focus.

I hope this book has been helpful. If you find yourself in the position of having to address a district committee or a Standing Committee, this book hopefully provided you with some insight into the proper preparation for the hearing/meeting. The way you can help me is by sharing your experiences and insights with me. Feel free to call or email me with comments, questions, suggestions or any insight.

Phone: 313-821-5904

Email: tadatlaw@gmail.com.

APPENDIX A

UNOFFICIAL VERSION OF THE RULES

FOR THE MOST UP TO DATE RULES, GO TO:
www.michbar.org

STATE BAR OF MICHIGAN STANDING COMMITTEE ON
CHARACTER AND FITNESS RULES OF PROCEDURE
As Amended October 5, 2007

A. Application Processing.

1. An applicant shall complete and file with the State Bar an Affidavit of Personal History on forms required by the Committee. An investigation of the applicant may occur and documents and additional materials may be requested or obtained by staff assigned to assist the Standing and District Committees in the discharge of their duties.

2. Affidavits which are not properly executed and notarized, in which questions have been left unanswered, or which are not accompanied by the correct fees and a signed fingerprint card, or scanning receipt, whichever is applicable, shall be returned to the applicant without processing.

3. For each applicant whose investigation reveals significant adverse factual information, State Bar staff shall prepare a Notice of Referral in a form required by the Committee setting forth all adverse information revealed in the investigation. The Notice of Referral shall set forth with specificity the items which will form the basis of the interview, identify the District Committee Chairperson, and advise the applicant of the burden of proof, the applicant's right to counsel, to call witnesses and to present evidence.

4. The Notice of Referral shall be mailed to the applicant and to the District Committee Chairperson where the interview will be held. The copy of the Notice of Referral sent to the District Committee shall be accompanied by all investigative file materials.

5. If an applicant has criminal charges pending, the District Committee referral should be delayed until the pending proceeding is concluded. An applicant may request that a referral be made prior to the final adjudication of criminal charges, and the request should be granted provided that a District Committee report and recommendation does not issue until the criminal matter is concluded.

6. An applicant's failure to timely respond to requests for information will result in the file being closed. A file closed for failure to respond may not be reopened until the expiration of three years or such lesser period of time as determined by the Committee for good cause shown. A fee of $200 shall be charged to reopen any file closed for non-cooperation or following a

withdrawal of the application, or following a deferred decision of the Committee for more than a year.

7. An applicant's objection to providing information requested shall be included in the referral to a District Committee pursuant to Rule 15, Sec 1 (5)(b). If a District Committee has already rendered a report and recommendation prior to the applicant's objection to providing the requested information, the applicant's objection shall be scheduled for hearing by the Standing Committee pursuant to Rule 15, Sec 1{5)(f). If the information the applicant objects to providing is material to a determination of the applicant's current character and fitness to be recommended for admission, or if the applicant's refusal to provide the information materially obstructs the investigation so as to prevent a determination regarding the applicant's current character and fitness from being made, the applicant shall not be recommended for admission.

B. District Committee Proceedings.

1. An applicant is entitled to be represented by counsel of choice at any time during the proceedings. Upon receipt of written notice that a lawyer represents an applicant, or upon appearance of counsel at any proceeding concerning the applicant, all further communications regarding the applicant matter shall be conducted through applicant's counsel.

2. The District Committee Chairperson may request that State Bar staff conduct additional investigation of any matter, or may have the District Committee members undertake additional investigation. If the District Committee conducts additional investigation, all investigative materials shall be returned to the State Bar with the District Committee report.

3. If additional investigation results in additions or amendments to the Notice of Referral, the applicant wilt be given at least 10 days notice of the amended referral items.

4. The scope of the District Committee interview is determined by the Notice of Referral and by matters raised during questioning.

5. Within 10 days of receipt of an applicant referral, the District Committee Chairperson shall contact the applicant to set an interview date and to identify the District Committee members assigned to the matter. Disqualification of District Committee members shall be determined by the District Committee Chairperson under the guidelines of MCR 2.003. The District Committee Chairperson shall notify State Bar staff of the interview date. Once an interview is set, one adjournment of the interview date may be granted at the discretion of the District Committee Chairperson for good cause.

6. All proceedings before the District Committee shall be recorded.

7. Within 10 days after the conclusion of the interview, the District Committee shall forward to the State Bar a report and recommendation in a form prescribed by the Standing Committee. If a District Committee is unable to comply with the filing deadline, the District Committee Chairperson shall contact the Standing Committee Chairperson through State Bar staff to explain the delay.

8. The report and recommendation should address each matter in the Notice of Referral specifically and indicate the District Committee's findings and determination. The report should indicate whether the District Committee believes the applicant does or does not

currently possess the requisite good moral character and fitness to be admitted to practice law. All files and materials relating to the applicant shall be forwarded to the State Bar with the report and recommendation.

9. The recommendation of a District Committee is not binding upon the Standing Committee.

C. Prehearing Conferences.

1. The State Bar staff assigned to assist the Standing Committee, in addition to conducting investigations, shall also:

   a) review each report of a District Committee and advise the Standing Committee (1) whether each issue in the Notice of Referral has been addressed, (2) whether additional information has been received which was not a part of the District Committee report, and (3) whether the recommendation is consistent with previous determinations of the Standing Committee and the State Board of Law Examiners regarding similar conduct;

   b) provide nonbinding analysis and recommendations regarding referral matters to the District or Standing Committee; and

   c) perform any other task assigned by the Standing Committee to assist the District and Standing Committee in the discharge of their duties. The Standing Committee shall take action on the District Committee report at any scheduled meeting, or the members may vote by mail ballot or email ballot. If the Standing Committee determines that a hearing should be held, the applicant shall be notified in writing within ten days of the Standing Committee determination.

2. Within ten days of receipt of an applicant's request for or the Standing Committee's determination for a formal hearing, the State Bar staff shall designate a Committee member to preside at the applicant's hearing, designate from among the associate members of the Committee a counsel to act for the State Bar in the matter, and send the designee all information in the Character and Fitness Department's possession concerning the applicant, with the exception of the confidential tape recordings of the District Committee interview, absent a showing of good cause upon motion to the Presiding Committee Member, and a draft Proposed Prehearing Order.

3. The State Bar staff shall promptly send written notice to the applicant of:

   a. the name, address and telephone number of the Committee member who shall preside at a prehearing conference in the matter;

   b. the name, address and telephone number of designated State Bar Counsel;

   c. a copy of these rules;

   d. notice that all future communications should be directed to State Bar Counsel and the Presiding Committee Member.

4. Upon written request and upon advance payment of the per page copy fee in effect, the applicant or applicant's counsel will be provided a copy of all information in the Character and Fitness Department's possession concerning the applicant with the exception of the

following materials: work product; addresses and phone numbers of witnesses who request that this information be kept confidential; and confidential tape recordings of District Committee interviews, absent a showing of good cause upon motion to the Presiding Committee Member. In person review of information and materials in the Character and Fitness Department's possession is not permitted. Upon showing of extreme and adverse financial hardship and upon discretion of the Chair of the Standing Committee, fees may be reduced or waived.

5. The applicant may obtain subpoenas of witnesses or documents by submitting a request to the Presiding Committee Member, with a copy to the State Bar staff and to State Bar Counsel, sufficiently identifying the witness or document sought and briefly stating the relevance of the witness's testimony or the document to the application matter. State Bar Counsel may obtain subpoenas of witnesses or documents by submitting a request to the Presiding Committee Member, with a copy to the State Bar staff and the applicant, sufficiently identifying the witness or document sought and briefly stating the relevance of the witness's testimony or the document to the application matter. Subpoenas for State Bar Counsel shall be prepared by State Bar staff and issued by the Presiding Committee Member unless the Presiding Committee Member determines the request is improper or wholly without merit. The Presiding Member or State Bar staff shall send the issued subpoenas to the requesting party, who shall be responsible for serving the subpoenas pursuant to MCR 2.506(G).

6. State Bar Counsel and the applicant shall make every effort to stipulate to issues and exhibits prior to the prehearing conference. State Bar Counsel and the applicant may obtain testimony of named witnesses through deposition, a transcript of which shall be accepted by the Standing Committee as an exhibit in lieu of direct testimony; costs of the transcripts shall be paid by the calling party. Any exhibits which are not stipulated may be offered as evidence in the course of the hearing.

7. Within 30 days of the designation of the Presiding Committee Member and State Bar Counsel, State Bar Counsel shall file with the Presiding Committee Member, with a copy to the applicant and the State Bar staff, a Proposed Prehearing Order setting forth the issues to be addressed at the hearing, accompanied by a proposed witness list and proposed exhibits. The applicant shall have 15 days to file with the Presiding Committee Member, with a copy to State Bar Counsel and the State Bar staff, any stipulation as to issues, witnesses and exhibits, any proposed witnesses and exhibits, and any motions or objections to the Proposed Prehearing Order.

8. Within 15 days of receipt of the applicant's response to the Proposed Prehearing Order, the Presiding Committee Member through State Bar staff shall schedule a prehearing conference by phone or in person to resolve any outstanding issues, hear and rule on motions, finalize the Prehearing Order, determine the amount of hearing time that should be scheduled, and schedule a date for the hearing. The applicant and State Bar Counsel may present motions, ask for rulings, and request subpoenas. The decision of the Presiding Committee Member regarding the contents of the Prehearing Order shall be final.

9. The Prehearing Order shall be issued as soon as practicable after the prehearing conference, and forwarded to the State Bar staff. The Prehearing Order shall set forth the issues to be considered at the hearing, the stipulated exhibits, the witnesses, whether or not the applicant

will accept voting by associate members, or waive the quorum requirement, and the date, time and place of the hearing.

10. As soon as possible after receipt of the Prehearing Order, but in no event later than 10 days before the scheduled hearing, the State Bar staff shall provide written notice to State Bar Counsel and the applicant of the date, time and place of the hearing, and the applicant's right to be represented by counsel. The Prehearing Order and any rules to be followed in the proceedings shall be enclosed in the hearing notice.

11. The State Bar staff shall arrange for copies of the Prehearing Order, stipulated exhibits, and deposition transcripts to be marked and circulated to Standing Committee members scheduled to hear the matter as soon as practicable, but in no case less than 10 days prior to the hearing date. Any evidence which is not circulated by the State Bar staff shall be presented at the hearing upon motion of the applicant or State Bar Counsel.

D. Standing Committee Proceedings.

1. Upon arrival at the hearing site, the applicant and State Bar Counsel shall register with hearing staff and identify any witnesses who are expected for the hearing. Witnesses shall remain outside the hearing room until their testimony is called. Hearing attendees shall be limited to members of the Standing Committee, the applicant (and counsel, if any), State Bar Counsel, counsel assistants, State Bar staff, and a court reporter, unless the Presiding Committee Member has previously granted permission for other persons to be in attendance.

2. A quorum consists of five regular members of the Committee. An applicant may waive the quorum and also stipulate to voting by associate members of the Committee. When a hearing is continued, and the same Committee members cannot be present at both sessions, Committee members shall be required to review the record of the proceedings not attended prior to being allowed to vote on the matter. If the applicant objects to participation by a Committee member who has not been present during the entire proceedings, the member shall be excluded from questioning and voting.

3. The burden is upon the applicant to establish the applicant's good moral character and general fitness to warrant admission to the bar by clear and convincing evidence. The hearing shall proceed with presentation of the applicant's evidence and cross-examination by State Bar Counsel, followed by presentation by State Bar Counsel and cross-examination by the applicant, and finally questioning by the Committee members.

4. At the conclusion of the evidence and questioning, the Committee members will meet in executive session to attempt to reach a determination of the matter. The finding of a majority of those present and voting shall be the decision and recommendation of the Committee. If a resolution is reached in executive session, the Committee has the discretion to verbally advise the applicant of the decision. If a resolution is not reached in executive session, the Presiding Committee Member shall either schedule a telephone conference call among Committee members to be held after receipt of the transcript of the proceedings, shall order additional investigation or additional recorded proceedings, or shall order briefs or supplemental filings from the applicant and State Bar Counsel. If additional investigation, proceedings, or filings are required, the applicant and State Bar Counsel shall be advised.

5. A Committee member will be assigned by the Presiding Committee Member to draft an opinion in a form prescribed by the Committee. The opinion shall address each item in the Prehearing Order and set forth findings and the Committee's determination. The draft opinion shall be circulated within 14 days to each member voting on the matter for comment. Failure to respond with comments is deemed approval by the committee of the opinion. Any comments received shall be resolved by consultation between the Presiding Committee Member and the drafter.

6. The opinion shall be forwarded to the applicant and to the State Board of Law Examiners within 30 days of the Committee's decision. The opinion forwarded to the State Board of Law Examiners shall be accompanied by the Prehearing Order, the transcript of the Standing Committee proceedings in the case of a denial or split decision, and the exhibits presented at the Standing Committee proceedings.

7. If a hearing is held before the State Board of Law Examiners, the applicant (through counsel, if any). State Bar Counsel, and the State Bar staff shall be notified. A State Bar Counsel shall be designated by State Bar staff if previous State Bar Counsel is unavailable, and shall be prepared to proceed as if before the Standing Committee, regardless of the Standing Committee decision in the matter.

E. Miscellaneous

1. Time frames stated in these rules should be treated as goals and not as affording any rights to any person for failing to meet any particular time frame. Michigan Rules of Evidence and Michigan Rules of Civil Procedure may be considered as guidelines for these proceedings, but are not binding.

2. Rulings of the Presiding Committee Member regarding motions, procedure, admissibility of evidence, and interpretations of these rules are final.

3. The revelation or discovery of any of the following conduct should be treated as cause for further inquiry and considered when a district or standing Committee makes a recommendation, included, but not limited to:
   - unlawful conduct
   - academic misconduct
   - making of false statements, including omissions
   - misconduct in employment
   - acts involving dishonesty, fraud, deceit or misrepresentation
   - abuse of legal process
   - neglect of financial responsibilities
   - neglect of professional obligations
   - violation of an order of a court
   - evidence of mental or emotional instability
   - evidence of drug or alcohol dependency
   - denial of admission to the bar in another jurisdiction on character and fitness grounds
   - activities which constitute practicing law without the benefit of licensure
   - disciplinary actions by a lawyer disciplinary agency or other professional disciplinary agency of any jurisdiction.

4. The following factors may be considered when assigning weight and significance to applicant's prior conduct, but not limited to:

    -   the applicant's age at the time of the conduct
    -   the recency of the conduct
    -   the seriousness of the conduct
    -   the reliability of the information concerning the conduct
    -   the factors underlying the conduct
    -   the cumulative effect of conduct or information
    -   the evidence of rehabilitation
    -   the applicant's positive social contributions since the conduct
    -   the applicant's candor in the admissions process
    -   the materiality of any omissions or misrepresentations
    -   affirmative efforts to rectify situation or prevent a recurrence
    -   timeliness of the cooperation with application and investigation process

5. An Applicant must successfully meet the general requirements for admission to the practice of law as set forth in the Rules for the Board of Law Examiners. In addition, in order to be recommended for admission by the Standing Committee on Character and Fitness and Fitness, the Applicant must demonstrate he or she:

    a. Will exercise good judgment, both ethically and professionally, on behalf of clients or oneself when conducting business and when engaging in financial dealings;
    b. Will avoid illegal, dishonest, fraudulent or deceitful conduct in one's personal and professional relationships and with respect to one's legal obligations;
    c. Will avoid acts which exhibit disregard for health, safety, welfare and rights of others;
    d. Will conduct oneself with respect for and in accordance with the law; and
    e. Will conduct oneself professionally and in a manner that engenders respect for the law and the profession.

APPENDIX B

Michigan Supreme Court
BOARD OF LAW EXAMINERS
Michigan Hall of Justice
P.O. Box 30052 Lansing, MI 48909
Phone (517)373-4453 <u>ble-info@courts.mi.gov</u>

<u>For the latest version of the Board's Policies and procedures, go to</u>:
http://courts.mi.gov/courts/michigansupremecourt/ble/pages/default.aspx

UNOFFICIAL VERSION – FOR REFERENCE ONLY

Rules, Statutes, and Policy Statements

September 2013

Table of Contents

Introduction

These Policy Statements are a memorialization of the practices, policies, and procedures adopted by the Board of Law Examiners. Each Policy Statement is numbered to correspond with the rule or statute it implements.

These Policy Statements do not constitute legal advice and are not officially sanctioned by the Michigan Supreme Court. They implement the Rules of the Board of Law Examiners, statutory mandates, and the practices, policies, and procedures of the Board of Law Examiners. They do not confer any procedural or substantive due process rights and are subject to change at any time without notice.

Rule 1. General Requirements

An applicant for admission to the practice of law must:

A. Be 18 years old or older;
B. Possess good moral character; and
C. Have completed, before entering law school, at least 60 semester hours or 90 quarter hours toward an undergraduate degree from an accredited school or while attending an accredited junior or community college.

Policy Statements

1(B)-1. *Good Moral Character*

An applicant for admission to the practice of law must be of good moral character. This requirement is contained in the Board's rules and MCL 600.934, which refers to MCL 338.41. That statute defines "good moral character" as the propensity on the part of the person to serve the public in a fair, honest, and open manner. The Board considers "fair" to mean legitimately sought, done, given, etc., for example, proper under the rules; courteous; civil; in a fair manner. The Board also considers the standards contained in the Rules of Procedure of the Standing Committee on Character and Fitness, in particular Rule E(5), which states:

> An applicant must successfully meet the general requirements for admission to the practice of law as set forth in the Rules for the Board of Law Examiners. In addition, in order to be recommended for admission by the Standing Committee on Character and Fitness, the applicant must demonstrate that he or she will:
>
> a. Exercise good judgment, both ethically and professionally, on behalf of clients or oneself when conducting business and when engaging in financial dealings;
> b. Avoid illegal, dishonest, fraudulent or deceitful conduct in one's personal and professional relationships and with respect to one's legal obligations;
> c. Avoid acts which exhibit disregard for health, safety, welfare and rights of others;
> d. Conduct oneself with respect for and in accordance with the law; and
> e. Conduct oneself professionally and in a manner that engenders respect for the law and the profession.

1(B)-2. *Good Moral Character—Burden of Proof*

The applicant has the burden of demonstrating good moral character by clear and convincing evidence.

Rule 2. Admission by Examination

A. An application must be filed by November 1 for the February examination, or March 1 for the July examination. Late applications will be accepted until December 15 for the February examination, or May 15 for the July examination. An application must be accompanied by payment of the fee. All materials filed are confidential.

B. Before taking the examination, an applicant must obtain a JD degree from a reputable and qualified law school that:

1. Is incorporated in the United States, its territories, or the District of Columbia; and

2. Requires for graduation, 3 school years of study for full-time students, and 4 school years of study for part-time or night students. A school year must be at least 30 weeks.

   a. A law school approved by the American Bar Association is reputable and qualified. Other schools may ask the Board to approve the school as reputable and qualified. In the event the law school has ceased operations since an applicant's graduation, the request for approval may be made by the applicant. The Board may in its discretion permit applicants who do not possess a JD degree from an ABA-approved law school to take the examination based upon factors including, but not limited to, relevant legal education, such as an LLM degree from a reputable and qualified law school, and experience that otherwise qualifies the applicant to take the examination.

C. The State Bar character and fitness committee will investigate each applicant. The applicant must disclose any criminal conviction which carries a possible penalty of incarceration in jail or prison that has not been reversed or vacated and comply with the committee's requirements and requests. The committee will report the results of its investigation to the Board. If the committee report shows that an applicant lacks the necessary character and fitness, the Board will review the application, record, and report. If the Board accepts the report, the applicant is entitled to a hearing before the Board and may use the Board's subpoena power. The Board may permit an applicant to take the examination before the character and fitness committee reports. The Board will release the applicant's grade if character and fitness committee approval is obtained.

D. Every applicant for admission must achieve a passing score, as determined by the Board, on the Multistate Professional Responsibility Examination.

E. The Board may permit an applicant entering the armed forces before the examination immediately following graduation to take an earlier examination. The applicant must have completed, before the examination, 2 1/2 years full-time or 3 1/2 years part-time study. The Board will release the applicant's grade when the school certifies the applicant's graduation.

F. The applicant is responsible for meeting all requirements before the examination. The Board may act on information about an applicant's character whenever the information is received.

Policy Statements

2(A)-1. *Filing Deadlines and Fees*

Application deadlines are strictly enforced. Applications must be postmarked by the referenced date. The fees must be paid by money order, cashier's check, or certified check. All fees are nonrefundable. Applicants seeking accommodations under the Americans with Disabilities Act are held to the same deadlines for submitting those requests. The Board does not waive the examination requirement for medical or other reasons.

2(A)-2. *Limitation on Number of Applications*

There is no limit on the number of times an applicant can sit for the examination.

2(B)(1)-1. *Legal Education*

Applicants must have a JD from a reputable and qualified law school that is incorporated in the United States, its territories, or the District of Columbia. Law schools approved by the American Bar Association are reputable and qualified. To qualify, the law school must be fully or provisionally approved on the date the applicant's degree was conferred. Applications received from individuals not meeting this requirement are returned.

2(B)(1)-2. *Law School Certification*

Applicants are required to attest to the fact they have graduated with a JD from a reputable and qualified law school. The examination results of applicants taking the exam without first having so graduated are void.

2(B)(1)-3. *Board Approval of Law Schools*

Law schools not approved by the ABA may ask the Board to approve the school as reputable and qualified. The Board is not required to undertake the approval process in response to such a request. The Board has adopted the Standards for Approval of Law Schools (including Interpretations, Rules of Procedure and fee structure) promulgated by the Section of Legal Education and Admissions to the Bar of the American Bar Association, unless otherwise required by context, statute, court rule or Board policy. Any school seeking approval must pay the actual expenses of the Board incurred in making the determination whether the school is reputable and qualified. This includes, but is not limited to, the salaries of the necessary and appropriate persons to conduct the inspection, prepare a report and make a recommendation to the Board.

2(B)(2). *Graduates of Non-Approved Law Schools*

The Board may in its discretion permit applicants who do not possess a JD from an ABA-approved law school to take the examination. In making that determination, the Board looks to, among other things, relevant legal education and experience that otherwise qualifies the applicant to take the examination. The Board considers the quality of the law school(s) attended, existing accreditation, prior accreditation history or attempts at accreditation, and evidence of experience in the full-time practice of law.

Applicants must petition the Board of Law Examiners for a waiver of the Rule. The petition may take the form of a letter. A hearing or personal interview is not held. Good cause for a waiver must be shown by clear and convincing evidence. In order for the Board to evaluate whether it should grant a waiver, the Board requires individuals seeking a waiver to provide certain material. The Board uses this information in evaluating whether the individual may take the bar examination. The following must be provided:

a. College and law school transcripts (translated to English if necessary).

b. A detailed description of the applicant's legal education and training. This must include a syllabus from each of the courses taken, a list of the textbooks used, the attendance requirements at the time the applicant matriculated, and the number of credit hours required for graduation.

c. Descriptions of academic and professional records of all faculty and executive administrators of each law school attended.

d. Copies of all material being sent to applicants by the law school and the school catalog, class schedules and course descriptions.

e. Bar examination results, i.e., percent passed/failed, of graduates of the law school, classified by state administering the exam, for the previous three years.

f. A statement of whether the applicant has applied to take the bar exam in any other jurisdiction and the result of that request, and the result of any bar examination taken by the applicant.

g. A description of the applicant's work history.

h. Evidence of experience in the full-time practice of law. Such evidence should include, but is not limited to, a sworn affidavit detailing the nature and extent of the applicant's legal work experience during the time the applicant claims to have engaged in the fulltime practice of law; legal memoranda prepared by the applicant; copies of published cases resulting from pleadings and papers filed by the applicant in his or her capacity as an attorney; and/or letters of reference from the bench and bar in the jurisdiction in which the applicant has been engaged in the practice of law.

i. In the case of applicants with a law degree from a non-U.S. jurisdiction, a description of that country's legal system, including, but not limited to, whether the English common law substantially forms the basis of that country's jurisprudence and whether English is the language of instruction and practice in the courts of that jurisdiction.

j. A narrative statement as to why the applicant feels that good cause by clear and convincing evidence has been established.

k. Any other documentation, material, or information the applicant feels is relevant to the establishment of good cause.

l. The Board may request additional evidence as it deems appropriate. Material submitted to the Board is not returned to the applicant.

The Board has determined that applicants who specifically relied on the former rule, which granted eligibility to applicants with an LLM from a reputable and qualified law school, will be allowed to sit for the examination. Simply starting an LLM program before the June 30, 2004 effective date of the rule change, however, is not sufficient. If an applicant is relying on receipt of an LLM as part of the basis for granting a waiver, the degree must have already been conferred because the Board does not issue advisory opinions or rulings.

2(C)-1. *Duration of Character and Fitness Clearance*

Character and fitness clearance is valid for three years. The three-year period begins with the exam first applied for by the applicant, regardless of when clearance is obtained and whether the applicant actually sat for that examination. For example, an applicant applying for the February 2005 examination and receiving character and fitness clearance, would need to be reapproved before being allowed to sit for the February 2008 examination. Applicants not passing the examination within three years after receiving clearance must again be approved by the State Bar Standing Committee on Character and Fitness.

2(C)-2. *Character and Fitness Hearings*

Character and fitness hearings are heard de novo. They are confidential proceedings. The applicant has the burden of proving by clear and convincing evidence that he or she has the requisite character and fitness to practice law. The Michigan Rules of Evidence are considered as guidelines but are not binding. If the parties agree, the hearing can be limited to an appeal consisting of briefs and argument or a limited testimonial hearing. All evidence is taken under oath before a court reporter, although the parties may stipulate to present testimony by telephone. The applicant may be represented by counsel.

2(C)-3. *Review of Board's Decision/Reapplication*

There are no motions for rehearing or reconsideration of decisions made following character and fitness hearings. Review is by complaint for superintending control filed in the Supreme Court. Applicants denied character and fitness certification by the Board may not reapply for certification for two years after the denial. The Board may extend that period to up to five years. In that case, the Board's opinion will specify the reasons for imposition of the longer time period. The Board may impose a waiting period shorter than two years. Applicants must reapply to the Standing Committee, not the Board.

2(D). *Multistate Professional Responsibility Examination*

Beginning with the July 2009 bar examination, applicants taking the examination as first- time takers must receive a scaled score of 85 on the Multistate Professional Responsibility Examination. That score is valid indefinitely. For applicants taking the July 2009 bar examination as a re-examinee or as a transferee from a prior exam, the passing scaled score will remain at 75. If such a re-examinee or transferee fails the July 2009 examination, the passing scaled MPRE score will remain at 75.

2(E). *No Repeat Examinations without Character and Fitness and MPRE Clearance*

Applicants are allowed to take the bar examination one time only before character and fitness and MPRE clearance is received. Applicants failing the exam who do not have both clearances at the time exam scores are released receive unofficial results only, which allows them to participate in the appeal process. They do not receive an application for re-examination and cannot file an application for re-examination until both clearances are received.

Rule 3. Examination Subjects and Grading

A. The examination consists of two sections:

1. The Multistate Bar Examination prepared by the National Conference of Bar Examiners and administered on dates and under regulations set by the Conference.

2. An essay examination prepared by or under the supervision of the Board or by law professors selected by the Board, on these subjects:

    a. Real and personal property
    b. Wills and trusts
    c. Contracts
    d. Constitutional law
    e. Criminal law and procedure
    f. Corporations, partnerships, and agency
    g. Evidence
    h. Creditor's rights, including mortgages, garnishments and attachments
    i. Practice and procedure, trial and appellate, state and federal
    j. Equity
    k. Torts (including no-fault)
    l. The sales, negotiable instruments, and secured transaction articles of the Uniform Commercial Code
    m. Michigan Rules of Professional Conduct
    n. Domestic Relations
    o. Conflicts of laws
    p. Worker's compensation

B. The National Conference of Bar Examiners will grade the multistate section. The Board or its agents will grade the essay section, with the Board having final responsibility. The Board will determine a method for combining the grades and select a passing score."

Policy Statements

3-1. *Date of Examination*

The exam is only administered on the last Tuesday and Wednesday of February and July.

3-2. *Bar Examination Conduct*

Bar examination and related conduct of bar applicants must be beyond reproach. Applicants are at all times to maintain a professional attitude toward other applicants, proctors, and other examination personnel. Conduct that results in a violation of security or disrupts the administration of the examination may result in immediate disqualification and ejection from the examination. Such conduct includes violation of the Board's Security Policy, cheating, failing to follow all rules and instructions governing the administration of the examination, or otherwise compromising the security or integrity of the bar examination.

3-3. *Examination Security Policy*

Applicants are not permitted to bring any items into the examination room other than a clear plastic food storage type bag (maximum size one gallon), which may only contain:

a. Admission Certificate
b. Government issued photo I.D.
c. Wallet
d. Keys
e. Earplugs (not the big earphone/headphone type)
f. Pens, pencils, and erasers
g. Medication and medical items
h. Facial tissue
i. Non-digital watch or timepiece
j. One clear plastic bottle of water/juice/soda per exam session

The following items are strictly prohibited and will not be permitted in the exam room or the testing area, which includes the examination room, rest rooms, and hallway:

a. Coats
b. Handbags
c. Purses
d. Hats, hoods, or any other headgear (except items of religious apparel)
e. Backpacks
f. Duffle bags
g. Briefcases
h. Tote bags
i. Notes
j. Scratch paper
k. Books, magazines, newspapers, or any other reading material
l. Bar review or other study material in any format or media
m. Electronic devices, such as cell phones, calculators, pagers, cameras, radios, recording devices, hand-held computers, any type of personal digital assistant, wireless email devices, etc.
n. IPODs or similar devices
o. Headphones or headsets
p. Imaging devices
q. Any type of wireless communication device
r. Weapons of any kind, regardless of whether you have a permit to carry
s. Any other item not specifically allowed

Applicants must be prepared to demonstrate that their clothing does not contain prohibited items.

Applicants are cautioned that it is best not to even bring the prohibited items to the examination site because they will not be permitted into the examination room and there will be no place to store them. The Board is not responsible for the loss or damage to personal property, so it is strongly recommended that any such items be left at home, in the applicant's hotel room, or vehicle.

Possession of a prohibited device or item at the examination will be treated as a cheating incident and the applicant may be immediately disqualified and ejected from the examination.

3-4-1. *Accommodations Under the Americans with Disabilities Act*

Accommodations are available upon a showing that the applicant has a disability or medical condition warranting such accommodations. The Board employs the Americans with Disabilities Act standard, i.e., that a person is disabled if that individual has "a physical or mental impairment that substantially limits one or more of the major life activities of such individual." See Gonzales v National Board of Medical Examiners, 225 F3d 620 (CA 6, 2000). A "Special Accommodations Questionnaire and Affidavit" is available from the Board. The request must be filed not later than May 15 for the July examination and not later than December 15 for the February examination. These deadlines are strictly enforced. Upon receipt of a request for accommodations under the ADA, the Executive Director determines whether the request meets the requirements listed below. If it does not, it is returned and the applicant is given the opportunity to supplement the request. This does not operate, however, to extend any filing deadlines. In other words, it is the responsibility of the applicant to have complete materials submitted by the applicable deadline. The request for accommodations is judged on what is received by that deadline.

3-4-2. *General ADA Accommodation Request Requirements*

The following guidelines are provided to assist the applicant in documenting the need for accommodation based on an impairment that substantially limits one or more major life activities. Documentation submitted in support of a request is referred to experts in the appropriate area of disability. To support a request for test accommodations, an applicant must submit the following:

A. Completed Special Accommodations Questionnaire and Affidavit.
B. A detailed, comprehensive written report describing the disability and its severity and justifying the need for the requested accommodations. The following characteristics are expected of all documentation submitted in support of a request for accommodations. The documentation must:

    1. State a specific diagnosis of the disability.

        a. The diagnostic taxonomies used by the current edition of the Diagnostic and Statistical Manual of the American Psychiatric Association (DSM-IV) are recommended.

    2. Be current.

        a. As the manifestations of a disability may vary over time and in different settings, in most cases an evaluation should have been conducted within the past three years.

3. Describe the specific diagnostic criteria and/or diagnostic tests used, including date(s) of evaluation, test results and a detailed interpretation of the test results.

   a. This description should include the specific results of diagnostic procedures and tests utilized and should include relevant educational, developmental, and medical history. Where appropriate, specific test scores should be reported to support the diagnosis.

   b. Diagnostic methods used should be appropriate to the disability and current professional practices within the field. Informal or non-standardized evaluations should be described in enough detail that other professionals could understand their role and significance in the diagnostic process.

4. Describe in detail the individual's limitations due to the diagnosed disability, i.e., a demonstrated impact on functioning vis-a-vis the bar examination and explain the relationship of the test results to the identified limitations resulting from the disability.

   a. The current functional impact on physical, perceptual and cognitive abilities should be fully described.

5. Recommend specific accommodations and/or assistive devices including a detailed explanation of why these accommodations or devices are needed and how they will reduce the impact of the identified functional limitations.

6. Establish the professional credentials of the evaluator that qualify him/her to make the particular diagnosis, including information about license or certification and specialization in the area of the diagnosis.

   a. The evaluator should present evidence of comprehensive training and direct experience in the diagnosis and treatment of adults in the specific area of disability.

C. If no prior accommodations have been provided, the qualified professional expert should include a detailed explanation as to why no accommodations were given in the past and why accommodations are needed now.

3-4-3. *ADA Accommodation Request Requirements Regarding Learning Disabilities*

For those seeking accommodations based on a learning disability or other cognitive disorder:

A. The evaluation must be conducted by a qualified professional. The diagnostician must have comprehensive training in the field of learning disabilities and must have comprehensive training and direct experience in working with an adult population.

B. Testing/assessment must be current. The determination of whether an individual is "significantly limited" in functioning is based on assessment of the current impact of the impairment.

C. Documentation must be comprehensive. Objective evidence of a substantial limitation in cognition or learning must be provided. At a minimum, the comprehensive evaluation should include the following:

1. A diagnostic interview and history taking. Relevant historical information regarding the individual's academic history and learning processes in elementary, secondary and postsecondary education should be investigated and documented. The report of assessment should include a summary of a comprehensive diagnostic interview that includes relevant background information to support the diagnosis. In addition to the candidate's self-report, the report of assessment should include:

   a. A description of the presenting problem(s)
   b. A developmental history
   c. Relevant academic history including results of prior standardized testing, reports of classroom performance and behaviors including transcripts, study habits and attitudes and notable trends in academic performance
   d. Relevant family history, including primary language of the home and current level of fluency in English
   e. Relevant psychosocial history
   f. Relevant medical history including the absence of a medical basis for the present symptoms
   g. Relevant employment history
   h. A discussion of dual diagnosis, alternative or coexisting mood, behavioral, neurological and/or personality disorders along with any history of relevant medication and current use that may impact the individual's learning
   i. Exploration of possible alternatives that may mimic a learning disability when, in fact, one is not present.

2. A psychoeducational or neuropsychological evaluation. The psychoeducational or neuropsychological evaluation must be submitted on the letterhead of a qualified professional and it must provide clear and specific evidence that learning or cognitive disability does or does not exist:

   a. The assessment must consist of a comprehensive battery of tests.
   b. A diagnosis must be based on the aggregate of test results, history and level of current functioning. It is not acceptable to base a diagnosis on only one or two subtests. Objective evidence of a substantial limitation to learning must be presented.
   c. Tests must be appropriately normed for the age of the patient and must be administered in the designated standardized manner.

3. Minimally, the domains to be addressed should include the following:

   a. Cognitive functioning. A complete cognitive assessment is essential with all subtests and standard scores reported. Acceptable measures include, but are not limited to: Wechsler Adult Intelligence Scale-III (WAIS-III); Woodcock Johnson Psycho Educational Battery—Revised: Tests of Cognitive Ability; Kaufman Adolescent and Adult Intelligence Test.

b. Achievement. A comprehensive achievement battery with all subtests and standard scores is essential. The battery must include current levels of academic functioning in relevant areas such as reading (decoding and comprehension) and mathematics. Acceptable instruments include, but are not limited to, the Woodcock-Johnson Psycho Educational Battery—Revised: Tests of Achievement; The Scholastic Abilities Test for Adults (SATA); Woodcock Reading Mastery Tests—Revised.

 i. Specific achievement tests are useful instruments when administered under standardized conditions and when interpreted within the context of other diagnostic information. The Wide Range Achievement Test-3 (WRAT-3) and the Nelson-Denny Reading Test are not comprehensive diagnostic measures of achievement and therefore neither is acceptable if used as the sole measure of achievement.

c. Information processing. Specific areas of information processing (e.g., short- and long-term memory, sequential memory, auditory and visual perception/processing, auditory and phonological awareness, processing speed, executive functioning, motor ability) must be assessed. Acceptable measures include, but are not limited to, the Detroit Tests of Learning Aptitude--Adult (DTLA-A), Wechsler Memory Scale-III (WMS-III), information from the Woodcock Johnson Psycho Educational Battery Revised: Tests of Cognitive Ability, as well as other relevant instruments that may be used to address these areas.

d. Other assessment measures. Other formal assessment measures or nonstandard measures and informal assessment procedures or observations may be integrated with the above instruments to help support a differential diagnosis or to disentangle the learning disability from co-existing neurological and/or psychiatric issues. In addition to standardized test batteries, non-standardized measures and informal assessment procedure may be helpful in determining performance across a variety of domains.

4. Actual test scores must be provided (standard scores where available).
5. Records of academic history should be provided. Relevant records detailing learning processes and difficulties in elementary, secondary and postsecondary education should be included. Such records as grade reports, transcripts, teachers' comments and the like will serve to substantiate self-reported academic difficulties in the past and currently.
6. A differential diagnosis must be reviewed and various possible alternative causes for the identified problems in academic achievement should be ruled out. The evaluation should address key constructs underlying the concept of learning disabilities and provide clear and specific evidence of the information processing deficit(s) and how these deficits currently impair the individual's ability to learn. No single test or subtest is a sufficient basis for a diagnosis. The differential diagnosis must demonstrate that:

a. Significant difficulties persist in the acquisition and use of listening, speaking, reading, writing or reasoning skills.

b. The problems being experienced are not primarily due to lack of exposure to the behaviors needed for academic learning or to an inadequate match between the individual's ability and the instructional demands.

7. A clinical summary must be provided. A well-written diagnostic summary based on a comprehensive evaluative process is a necessary component of the report. Assessment instruments and the data they provide do not diagnose; rather, they provide important data that must be integrated with background information, historical information and current functioning. It is essential then that the evaluator integrate all information gathered in a well-developed clinical summary. The following elements must be included in the clinical summary:

a. Demonstration of the evaluator's having ruled out alternative explanations for the identified academic problems as a result of poor education, poor motivation and/or study skills, emotional problems, attention problems and cultural or language differences.

b. Indication of how patterns in cognitive ability, achievement and information processing are used to determine the presence of a learning disability.

c. Indication of the substantial limitation to learning presented by the learning disability and the degree to which it impacts the individual in the context of the bar exam.

d. Indication as to why specific accommodations are needed and how the effects of the specific disability are mediated by the recommended accommodation(s).

i. Problems such as test anxiety, English as a second language (in and of itself), slow reading without an identified underlying cognitive deficit or failure to achieve a desired academic outcome are not learning disabilities and therefore are not covered under the Americans with Disabilities Act.

8. Each accommodation recommended by the evaluator must include a rationale.

The evaluator must describe the impact the diagnosed learning disability has on a specific major life activity as well as the degree of significance of this impact on the individual. The diagnostic report must include specific recommendations for accommodations and a detailed explanation as to why each accommodation is recommended. Recommendations must be tied to specific test results or clinical observations. The documentation should include any record of prior accommodation or auxiliary aids, including any information about specific conditions under which the accommodations were used and whether or not they were effective. However, a prior history of accommodation, without demonstration of a current need, does not in and of itself warrant the provision of a like accommodation. If no prior accommodation(s) has been provided, the qualified professional expert should include a detailed explanation as to why no accommodation(s) was used in the past and why accommodation(s) is needed at this time.

3-4-4. ADA Accommodation Request Requirements Regarding Attention- Deficit/Hyperactivity Disorder (ADHD)

For those applicants seeking accommodations based on Attention-Deficit/Hyperactivity Disorder (ADHD):

A. The evaluation must be conducted by a qualified diagnostician. Professionals conducting assessments and rendering diagnoses of ADHD must be qualified to do so. Comprehensive training in the differential diagnosis of ADHD and other psychiatric disorders and direct experience in diagnosis and treatment of adults is necessary. The evaluator's name, title and professional credentials, including information about license or certification as well as the area of specialization, employment and state in which the individual practices should be clearly stated in the documentation.

B. Testing/assessment must be current. The determination of whether an individual is "significantly limited" in functioning is based on assessment of the current impact of the impairment on the bar examination testing program.

C. Documentation necessary to substantiate the Attention Deficit/Hyperactivity Disorder must be comprehensive. Objective, relevant, historical information is essential. Information verifying a chronic course of ADHD symptoms from childhood through adolescence to adulthood, such as educational transcripts, report cards, teacher comments, tutoring evaluations, job assessments and the like are necessary.

D. The evaluator is expected to review and discuss DSM-IV diagnostic criteria for ADHD and describe the extent to which the patient meets these criteria. The report must include information about the specific symptoms exhibited and document that the patient meets criteria for longstanding history, impairment and pervasiveness.

E. A history of the individual's presenting symptoms must be provided, including evidence of ongoing impulsive/hyperactive or inattentive behaviors (as specified in DSM-IV) that significantly impair functioning in two or more settings.

F. The information collected by the evaluator must consist of more than self-report. Information from third-party sources is critical in the diagnosis of adult ADHD. Information gathered in the diagnostic interview and reported in the evaluation should include, but not necessarily be limited to, the following:

1. History of presenting attention symptoms, including evidence of ongoing impulsive/ hyperactive or inattentive behavior that has significantly impaired functioning over time.
2. Developmental history.
3. Family history for presence of ADHD and other educational, learning, physical or psychological difficulties deemed relevant by the examiner;
4. Relevant medical and medication history, including the absence of a medical basis for the symptoms being evaluated.
5. Relevant psychosocial history and any relevant interventions.
6. A thorough academic history of elementary, secondary and postsecondary education.
7. Review of psycheducational test reports to determine if a pattern of strengths or weaknesses is supportive of attention or learning problems.

8. Evidence of impairment in several life settings (home, school, work, etc.) and evidence that the disorder significantly restricts one or more major life activities.

9. Relevant employment history.

10. Description of current functional limitations relative to an educational setting and to the bar exam in particular that are presumably a direct result of the described problems with attention.

11. A discussion of the differential diagnosis, including alternative or coexisting mood, behavioral, neurological and/or personality disorders that may confound the diagnosis of ADHD.

12. Exploration of possible alternative diagnoses that may mimic ADHD.

G. Relevant assessment batteries. A neuropsychological or psychoeducational assessment may be necessary in order to determine the individual's pattern of strengths or weaknesses and to determine whether there are patterns supportive of attention problems. Test scores or subtest scores alone should not be used as the sole basis for the diagnostic decision. Scores from subtests on the Wechsler Adult Intelligence Scale-III (WAIS-III), memory functions tests, attention or tracking tests or continuous performance tests do not in and of themselves establish the presence or absence of ADHD. They may, however, be useful as one part of the process in developing clinical hypotheses. Checklists and/or surveys can serve to supplement the testing is used, standard scores must be provided for all normed measures.

H. Identification of DSM-IV Criteria. A diagnostic report must include a review of the DSM-IV criteria for ADHD both currently and retrospectively and specify which symptoms are present (see DSM-IV for specific criteria). According to DSM-IV, "the essential feature of ADHD is a persistent pattern of inattention and/or hyperactivity- impulsivity that is more frequent and severe than is typically observed in individuals at a comparable level of development." Other criteria include:

1. Symptoms of hyperactivity-impulsivity or inattention that cause impairment that were present in childhood.

2. Current symptoms that have been present for at least the past six months.

3. Impairment from the symptoms present in two or more settings (school, work, home).

I. Documentation must include a specific diagnosis. The report must include a specific diagnosis of ADHD based on the DSM-IV diagnostic criteria. Individuals who report problems with organization, test anxiety, memory and concentration only on a situational basis do not fit the prescribed diagnostic criteria for ADHD. Given that many individuals benefit from prescribed medications and therapies, a positive response to medication by itself is not supportive of a diagnosis, nor does the use of medication in and of itself either support or negate the need for accommodation.

J. A clinical summary must be provided. A well-written diagnostic summary based on a comprehensive evaluative process is a necessary component of the assessment. The clinical summary must include:

1. Demonstration of the evaluator's having ruled out alternative explanations for inattentiveness, impulsivity, and/or hyperactivity as a result of psychological or medical disorders or non-cognitive factors.

2. Indication of how patterns of inattentiveness, impulsivity and/or hyperactivity across the life span and across settings are used to determine the presence of ADHD.

3. Indication of the substantial limitation to learning presented by ADHD and the degree to which it impacts the individual in the context for which accommodations are being requested (e.g., impact on the bar exam).

4. Indication as to why specific accommodations are needed and how the effects of ADHD symptoms, as designated by the DSM-IV, are mediated by the accommodation(s).

K. Each accommodation recommended by the evaluator must include a rationale. The evaluator must describe the impact of ADHD (if one exists) on a specific major life activity as well as the degree of significance of this impact on the individual. The diagnostic report must include specific recommendations for accommodations. A detailed explanation must be provided as to why each accommodation is recommended and should be correlated with specific identified functional limitations. Prior documentation may have been useful in determining appropriate services in the past. However, documentation should validate the need for accommodations based on the individual's current level of functioning. The documentation should include any record of prior accommodation or auxiliary aid, including information about specific conditions under which the accommodation was used (e.g., standardized testing, final exams, subject exams, etc.) However, a prior history of accommodation without demonstration of a current need does not in and of itself warrant the provision of a similar accommodation. If no prior accommodation has been provided, the qualified professional and/or individual being evaluated should include a detailed explanation as to why no accommodation was used in the past and why accommodation is needed at this time. Because of the challenge of distinguishing ADHD from normal developmental patterns and behaviors of adults, including procrastination, disorganization, distractibility, restlessness, boredom, academic underachievement or failure, low self-esteem and chronic tardiness or in attendance, a multifaceted evaluation must address the intensity and frequency of the symptoms and whether these behaviors constitute impairment in a major life activity.

3(A)(1). *Day of Multistate Bar Examination*

The multistate bar examination is administered on the last Wednesday of February and July.

3(A)(2). *Day of Essay Examination*

The essay portion of the examination is administered on the Tuesday immediately preceding the last Wednesday of February and July and consists of 15 questions.

3(B). *Examination Scoring*

Each essay question has 10 possible points for a total of 150 possible points. After reading and considering each answer, the grader shall assign a score consistent with the following standards:

A. Score of 9-10

A Score of 9-10 demonstrates a high degree of competence in response to the question. While not reserved for a perfect answer, a 9-10 answer demonstrates a full understanding of the facts, a complete recognition of the issues presented and the applicable principles of law, and a good ability to reason to a conclusion. A 9-10 answer is clear, concise and complete. A score of 9 or 10 is not reserved for a perfect or near perfect answer. A score of 10 is not reserved for the single "best" answer that a grader may encounter to a particular question or on a particular examination. A grade of 10 may be assigned if the grader believes that the applicant has done an exceptional job considering the time and circumstances.

B. Score of 8

A score of 8 demonstrates clear competence in response to the question. An 8 answer demonstrates a fairly complete understanding of the facts, recognizes more of the issues and applicable law, and reasons fairly well to a conclusion.

C. Score of 7

A score of 7 demonstrates competence in response to the question. A 7 answer demonstrates an adequate understanding of the facts, an adequate recognition of most of the issues and law, and adequate ability to reason to a conclusion.

D. Score of 5-6

A score of 5-6 demonstrates some competence in response to the question but is inadequate. A 5-6 answer demonstrates a weak understanding of the facts, misses significant issues, fails to recognize applicable law, and demonstrates inadequate reasoning ability.

E. Score of 4

A score of 4 demonstrates only limited competence in response to the question and is seriously flawed. A 4 answer demonstrates little understanding of the facts or law and little ability to reason to a conclusion.

F. Score of 1-3

A score of 1-3 demonstrates fundamental deficiencies in understanding facts and law. A 1-3 answer shows virtually no ability to reason or analyze.

G. A Score of 0

A score of zero should be assigned only when the applicant makes no attempt to answer the question, or when the answer shows no reasonable attempt to identify or address the issues raised by the question.

There are 200 possible points on the multistate portion. A combined score of 135 or above is necessary to pass the exam using the following formula:

Combined score = [(4/3)essay total + MBE score] / 2

A passing score is valid for three years. Applicants not becoming active members of the State Bar of Michigan within that time must retake and pass the examination.

Rule 4. Post-Examination Procedures

A. The Executive Director will release examination results at the Board's direction. Blue books will be kept for 3 months after results are released.
B. Within 30 days after the day the results are released, the applicant may ask the Board to reconsider the applicant's essay grades. The applicant shall file with the Executive Director two (2) copies of:

1. The request;
2. The answer given in the applicant's blue books; and
3. An explanation why the applicant deserves a higher grade.

C. An applicant for re-examination may obtain an application from the Executive Director. The application must be filed at least sixty (60) days before the examination. If the applicant's clearance is more than three (3) years old, the applicant must be approved by the State Bar Committee on Character and Fitness.

Policy Statements

4(A)-1. *Release of Results*

Results are released by first-class mail only. No telephone or other requests for results are honored. Applicants with character and fitness, MPRE, and law school certification receive official results. For those who passed the examination, official results include the Board's certification and information about how to apply for membership in the State Bar of Michigan. The Board's certification is valid for three years. For those who failed the examination, official results include an application for re-examination. Applicants missing character and fitness or MPRE clearance receive unofficial results and are eligible to participate in the appeal process. Applicants not having law school certification do not receive any results until certification is received. After a suitable time allowing for a reasonable opportunity for notification of applicants by mail, a list of certified passers is posted on the Board's website. Applicants must wait ten business days for the delivery of results. Applicants not receiving results after the ten-day period, must submit a written request to the Board of Law Examiners to receive a duplicate result packet. The request must include a statement that the applicant did not receive the original result packet, a statement promising to return the original result packet if received, and the applicant's full name, current address, and month and year he or she sat for the examination.

4(A)-2. *Copies of Bluebooks*

Applicants failing the exam may request copies of their bluebooks. Requests must be made in writing and be accompanied by $20 (money order or certified funds). Bluebooks are destroyed three months after results are released.

4(B). *Appeals*

Appeals must be postmarked by the date stated in the material received by applicants failing the exam. That date is 30 days from the date results are released, except when the due date would fall on a Sunday or other Court holiday. No exceptions are made to that deadline, although applicants who did not receive results because of a delay in the Board's receipt of law school certification are given 30 days from the date of the release of his or her examination results. The requirements listed in the appeal instructions are strictly enforced. Appeals not meeting those requirements are rejected. Essay answers are not re-read or otherwise regraded following an appeal. Any further review must be by complaint for superintending control filed in the Supreme Court.

4(C). *Applications for Re-examination*

Applications for re-examination are sent to those applicants who fail the exam along with their official results. Applicants receiving unofficial results do not receive an application for reexamination until official results are released. Character and fitness clearance is valid for three years. The three-year period begins with the exam first applied for by the applicant, regardless of when clearance is obtained and whether the applicant actually sat for that examination. For example, an applicant applying for the February 2005 examination and receiving character and fitness clearance, would need to be re-approved before being allowed to sit for the February 2008 examination. Applicants not passing the examination within three years after receiving clearance must again be approved by the State Bar Standing Committee on Character and Fitness.

Rule 5. Admission Without Examination

A. An applicant for admission without examination must:

1. Qualify under Rules 1 and 2(B).
2. Be licensed to practice law in the United States, its territories, or the District of Columbia.
3. Be a member in good standing of the Bar where admitted.
4. Intend to practice law in Michigan, or to be a full-time instructor in a reputable and qualified Michigan law school.
5. Have, after being licensed and for 3 of the 5 years preceding the application:

    a. Actively practiced law as a principal business or occupation in a jurisdiction where admitted (the practice of law under a special certificate pursuant to Rule 5[D] or as a special legal consultant pursuant to Rule 5[E] does not qualify as the practice of law required by this rule);
    b. Been employed as a full-time instructor in a reputable and qualified law school in the United States, its districts, or its territories; or
    c. Been on active duty (other than for training or reserve duty) in the United States armed forces as a judge advocate, legal specialist, or legal officer. The judge advocate general (or a comparable officer) or delegate must certify the assignment and the inclusive dates. The Supreme Court may, for good cause, increase the 5-year period. Active duty in the United

States armed forces not satisfying Rule 5(A)(5)(c) may be excluded when computing the 5-year period.

B. An applicant must submit the National Conference of Bar Examiners' Request for Preparation of a Character Report along with other material required by the Board and payment of the fees.

C. An applicant not satisfying Rule 5(A) will be notified and given an opportunity to appear before the Board. The applicant may use the Board's subpoena power.

D. An attorney:

1. Ineligible for admission without examination because of the inability to satisfy Rule 5(A)(5); and

2. Practicing law in an institutional setting, e.g., counsel to a corporation or instructor in a law school, may apply to the Board for a special certificate of qualification to practice law. The applicant must satisfy Rule 5(A)(1)-(3), and comply with Rule 5(B). The Board may then issue the special certificate, which will entitle the attorney to continue current employment if the attorney becomes an active member of the State Bar. If the attorney leaves the current employment, the special certificate automatically expires; if the attorney's new employment is also institutional, the attorney may reapply for another special certificate.

E. Special Legal Consultants

1. To qualify for admission without examination to practice as a special legal consultant one must:

    a. Be admitted to practice in a foreign country and have actually practiced, and be in good standing, as an attorney or counselor at law or the equivalent in such foreign country for at least 3 of the 5 years immediately preceding the application;

    b. Possess the good moral character and general fitness requisite for a member of the bar of this state;

    c. Fulfill the requirements of MCL 600.934 and 600.937;

    d. Be a resident of this or another state of the United States, its territories or the District of Columbia and maintain an office in this state for the practice of law; and

    e. Be over 18 years of age.

2. In considering whether to license an applicant to practice pursuant to Rule 5(E), the Board may in its discretion take into account whether a member of the bar of this state would have a reasonable and practical opportunity to establish an office for the giving of legal advice to clients in the applicant's country of admission (as referred to in Rule 5[E][a][1]), if there is pending with the Board a request to take this factor into account from a member of the bar of this state actively seeking to establish such an office in that country which raises a serious question as to the adequacy of the opportunity for such a member to establish such an office.

3. An applicant for a license as a special legal consultant shall submit to the Board:

a. A certificate from the authority in such foreign country having final jurisdiction over professional discipline, certifying as to the applicant's admission to practice and the date thereof and as to the good standing of such attorney or counselor at law or the equivalent, together with a duly authenticated English translation of such certificate if it is not in English;

b. A letter of recommendation from one of the judges of the highest law court or intermediate appellate court of such foreign country, together with a duly authenticated English translation of such letter if it is not in English;

c. The National Conference of Bar Examiners questionnaire and affidavit along with the payment of the requisite fee and such other evidence of the applicant's educational and professional qualifications, good moral character and general fitness, and compliance with the requirements of Rule 5(E)(a)(1)- (5) as the Board may require; and

d. Shall execute and file with the Executive Director of the State Board of Law Examiners, in such form and manner as the Board may prescribe:

    i. A duly acknowledged instrument in writing setting forth the special legal consultant's address in the state of Michigan and designating the Executive Director of the State Board of Law Examiners an agent upon whom process may be served, with like effect as if served personally upon the special legal consultant, in any action or proceeding thereafter brought against the special legal consultant and arising out of or based upon any legal services rendered or offered to be rendered by the special legal consultant within or to residents of the state of Michigan whenever after due diligence service cannot be made upon the special legal consultant at such address or at such new address in the state of Michigan as the special legal consultant shall have filed in the office of the Executive Director of the State Board of Law Examiners by means of a duly acknowledged supplemental instrument in writing; and

    ii. The special legal consultant's commitment to notify the Executive Director of the State Board of Law Examiners of any resignation or revocation of the special legal consultant's admission to practice in the foreign country of admission, or of any censure, suspension or expulsion in respect of such admission. Service of process on the Executive Director of the State Board of Law Examiners shall be made by personally delivering to and leaving with the Executive Director, or with a deputy or assistant authorized by the Executive Director to receive such service, at the Executive Director's office, duplicate copies of such process together with a fee of $10.00. Service of process shall be complete when the Executive Director has been so served. The Executive Director shall promptly send one of such copies to the special legal consultant to whom the process is directed, by certified mail, return receipt requested, addressed to such special legal consultant at the address specified by the special legal consultant as aforesaid.

4. A person licensed to practice as a special legal consultant must maintain active membership in the State Bar of Michigan and must discharge the responsibilities of state bar membership and is authorized to render professional legal advice:

    a. On the law of the foreign country where the legal consultant is admitted to practice.
    b. May use the title 'special legal consultant' either singly or in connection with the authorized title or firm name in the foreign country of the legal consultant's admission to practice, provided that in each case the name of such foreign country be identified.

Policy Statements

5. *Review of Applications for Admission without Examination*

Applications for admission without examination are initially reviewed by the Executive Director to determine if the materials facially meet the requirements of the Rule. If they do not, the materials are returned with an opportunity given for supplementation or explanation. Applicants not meeting the requirements of the Rule may seek a waiver of a particular provision for good cause. Good cause must be shown by clear and convincing evidence. In those situations, the issue is presented to the Board before the NCBE process begins and the applicant's funds are retained until the Board rules. Once the NCBE process begins, all funds become nonrefundable.

Applications facially meeting the requirements of the Rule are sent to the National Conference of Bar Examiners for preparation of a character report. If no irregularities are disclosed, the Executive Director approves the application and the applicant is sent the Board's certification. The certification is valid for three years.

5(A)(1)-1. *Good Moral Character*

An applicant for admission without examination must be of good moral character. The Board may refer an applicant to the Standing Committee on Character and Fitness for a report before granting the application. The applicant is responsible for any fees assessed by the Standing Committee. An applicant may file an application while there is a grievance pending against him or her, but the Board will not approve the application until any pending grievances are resolved. Favorable resolution of any grievance does not bar the Board from referring the applicant to the Standing Committee.

5(A)(1)-2. *Reputable and Qualified Law School*

An applicant for admission without examination must be a graduate of a law school deemed reputable and qualified at the time the applicant's degree was conferred. Applicants seeking a waiver of this requirement must supply the same material required of those applicants seeking to take the bar examination who do not have a qualifying JD

5(A)(2). *Licensure in Another Jurisdiction*

Licensure status is confirmed by the National Conference of Bar Examiners.

5(A)(3). *Member in Good Standing*

Good standing status is confirmed by the National Conference of Bar Examiners.

5(A)(4). *Intention to Practice in Michigan*

The applicant must state that he or she intends to practice law in Michigan or be a full- time instructor in a reputable and qualified law school in Michigan. The quantity of practice in Michigan is not set.

5(A)(5). *Duration of Practice in Another Jurisdiction*

Individuals must have practiced law for three of the five years preceding the application. For good cause, the Board may increase the five-year period.

5(A)(5)(a)-1. *Practice of Law*

To constitute a principal business or occupation, the practice of law in the other jurisdiction must have been greater than 50% of the applicant's time. The practice of law is defined as counseling or assisting another in matters that require the use of legal discretion and profound legal knowledge.

5(A)(5)(a)-2. *Jurisdiction Where Admitted*

The practice must have been in a U.S. jurisdiction where admitted. Practice in the federal courts in a state other than where admitted qualifies.

5(A)(5)(a)-3. *Judicial Clerks*

Employment as a judicial clerk will be considered the practice of law. For purposes of the requirement of Rule 5 that the practice of law must have been in a jurisdiction where admitted, in the case of federal judicial clerks, admission to a state bar will not be required. In the case of all other judicial clerks, the only time included in the determination of whether the applicant meets the three-years-in-five requirement will be the period of employment after licensure in that jurisdiction, i.e. the length of time the applicant practiced law in a jurisdiction where admitted.

5(A)(5)(a)-4. *Agency Practice*

Practice before an agency or tribunal that does not require law licensure does not satisfy the practice requirement.

5(B). *Fees*

Applications for admission without examination must be accompanied by a money order, cashier's check, or certified check in the amount of $600 made payable to the "State of Michigan" and a money order, cashier's check, or certified check in the amount of $375 made payable to the "National

Conference of Bar Examiners." Once the application materials are sent to the National Conference of Bar Examiners, all funds are nonrefundable.

5(C). *Hearing*

A request for a hearing must be made in writing within 60 days of the letter notifying the applicant of that option. Waivers of the provisions of Rule 5(A) are for good cause only, which must be shown by clear and convincing evidence.

5(D). *Special Certificates*

Only one special certificate is issued at a time. A special certificate automatically expires when the current employment is terminated. If an attorney's new employment is also institutional, another special certificate will be issued upon receipt of proof of that employment.

Rule 6. Fees

The fees are: an application for examination, $340 and an additional fee for the late filing of an application or transfer of an application for examination, $100; an application for reexamination, $240; an application for recertification, $200; an application for admission without examination, $600 plus the requisite fee for the National Conference of Bar Examiners' report. Checks must be payable to the State of Michigan.

Policy Statement

6.*Manner of Payment*

Funds must be paid by money order, cashier's check or certified check.

Rule 7. Exceptions

"An applicant may ask the Board to waive any requirement except the payment of fees. The applicant must demonstrate why the request should be granted."

Policy Statement

7.*Waivers of Rules.*

Waivers are granted for good cause only, which must be demonstrated by clear and convincing evidence. Carelessness, inattention, or willful disregard of the Board's processes do not constitute good cause. No motions for rehearing or reconsideration of Board decisions on requests for waivers will be accepted. Review is by complaint for superintending control filed in the Supreme Court. The Board does not issue advisory decisions.

Rule 8. Recertification

"An applicant for recertification shall file an application and other material required by the Board. After a hearing the Board shall either recertify the applicant or require that the applicant pass the examination described in Rule 3. An applicant may use the Board's subpoena power for the hearing. An applicant who is an inactive State Bar member or who had previously voluntarily resigned from the State Bar or who previously elected emeritus status, and who has been employed in another jurisdiction in one of the ways listed in Rule 5(A)(5) is entitled to recertification by the Board."

Policy Statements

8-1. *Recertification*

Rule 3 of the Rules Concerning the State Bar of Michigan requires persons who have been on inactive status for three years or more to be recertified by the Board before the person can be reclassified as an active member of the State Bar. Such a person must demonstrate that he or she possesses sufficient ability and learning in the law to enable the member to properly practice as an attorney and counselor in Michigan. Persons not meeting that standard must take and pass the bar examination in order to be recertified. Applications for recertification can be obtained from the Board's administrative assistant. The fee is $200, payable by money order, certified check, or cashier's check.

8-2. *Inactive Members of the State Bar*

An applicant for recertification who is an inactive State Bar of Michigan member and who has been employed in another jurisdiction in one of the ways listed in Rule 5(A)(5) will be recertified. Inactive members who have not been employed in another jurisdiction in one of the ways listed in Rule 5(A)(5) must demonstrate that they possess sufficient ability and learning in the law to enable the member to properly practice as an attorney and counselor in Michigan. The State Bar determines the amount of back dues that are required to be paid before readmission.

8-3. *Resigned or Emeritus Members of the State Bar*

An applicant for recertification who voluntarily resigned from the State Bar of Michigan or who voluntarily elected emeritus status, and who has been employed in another jurisdiction in one of the ways listed in Rule 5(A)(5) will be recertified. Such an applicant for recertification who does not meet the requirements of Rule 5(A)(5) must take and pass the bar examination.

8-5. *Character and Fitness*

In cases where the applicant's license was suspended or revoked and has been reinstated subject to being recertified, the Board relies on the finding of the Attorney Discipline Board and does not inquire into the applicant's character and fitness, unless that finding is more than three years old. In that situation, the applicant is referred to the State Bar for a character and fitness determination. The applicant is allowed to take the bar examination while that review is being conducted. The Board does not consider applications for recertification before the Attorney Discipline Board has determined the individual is eligible for reinstatement. An applicant may file an application while there is a grievance pending against him or her in another jurisdiction, but the Board will not approve the application until any pending grievances are resolved. Favorable resolution of any such grievance does not bar the Board from referring the applicant to the State Bar.

Statutes

MCL 600.922 Board of law examiners; membership, vacancies, officers.

"There is hereby constituted a board of law examiners consisting of 5 active members of the bar each of whom shall hold office for 5 years and 1 of whom shall be appointed by the governor on nomination by the supreme court on the first day of July in each year. Vacancies on the board shall be filled in like manner for the unexpired term. The president of the board is the member of the board whose term first expires. The board shall elect a secretary annually from its own membership. The clerk of the supreme court ex-officio is the assistant secretary and treasurer of the board. If a vacancy occurs in the office of president, the board may elect a president for the unexpired term from its own membership."

Policy Statement

922-1. *Executive Director and Assistant Secretary as Legal Counsel*

The Executive Director and Assistant Secretary serve as in-house legal counsel and provide legal advice to the Board, perform legal research and summarize past practices of the Board. In his or her role as legal counsel, the Executive Director and Assistant Secretary make recommendations on agenda items. The Board considers all of its communications with the Executive Director and Assistant Secretary to be attorney-client communications and therefore privileged.

MCL 600.925 Board of law examiners; applicants for admission; rules and regulations.

"The board of law examiners has charge of the investigation and examination of all persons who initially apply for admission to the bar of this state. The board may adopt suitable regulations, subject to approval by the supreme court, concerning the performance of its functions and duties. Regulations adopted pursuant to this section need not be published pursuant to Act No. 88 of the Public Acts of 1943, being sections 24.71 to 24.82, inclusive, of the Compiled Laws of 1948, as amended. The board has the power of subpoena, and the authority to administer oaths, and to take testimony under oath, which may be exercised by any member of the board in cases of applicants for admission to the bar."

Policy Statements

925-1. *Communications with Board Members by Applicants and/or Their Representatives*

The members of the Board of Law Examiners serve as fact-finders and otherwise act as the final authority on numerous issues relating to applicants for admission to the bar. It acts as a body and therefore communication of any type with board members by an applicant or an applicant's representative (legal or otherwise) relating to the applicant is not appropriate. Questions regarding the status of a matter, procedure, or other issue should be directed to the Executive Director. Members of the Board will not respond to communications except to refer the person to the Executive Director.

925-2. *Disqualification of Board Members*

When an issue of a board member's disqualification is raised, either by motion or otherwise, the issue will be addressed using the provisions of MCR 2.003, relating to Supreme Court justices, as a guide.

925-3. *Motions and Subpoenas*

While the Board has subpoena power, it is not within its power to adjudicate discovery motions based on alleged noncompliance with those subpoenas. Applicants must seek judicial relief to enforce a subpoena. The Board does not entertain motions for summary disposition.

MCL 600.928 Board of law examiners; meetings, quorum.

"The board of law examiners shall meet at least once in each year at such times and places as the chairman shall determine for the purpose of investigating, examining, hearing, and passing upon the qualifications of applicants for admission to the bar, and to transact such other business as may come before the board. Three members of the board shall constitute a quorum. The action of a majority of the members present at a meeting at which a quorum is present shall be the action of the board."

Policy Statements

928-1. *Board Meetings*

Board meetings are not open to the public.

928-2. *Meeting Agenda*

Due to the requirements of applicant confidentiality and because the agendas contain the Executive Director's and/or Assistant Secretary's recommendations as in-house counsel, agendas are privileged, not matters of public record, and not available for inspection.

928-3. *Minutes of Meetings*

The minutes of each meeting shall be prepared by the Executive Director and are to be approved at the next meeting. Board minutes contain privileged and otherwise confidential information and are not open to the public and are not available for inspection.

MCL 600.931 Fees for admission to bar; compensation and expenses of board of law examiners.

A. The fees required to be paid by each applicant for admission to the bar shall be paid to the board of law examiners, and shall be deposited in the general fund for the restricted purpose of expenditures of the supreme court related to the administration of the board of law examiners.

B. Subject to subsection (3), the fees described in this section are as follows:

1. The fee for applying for examination is $175.00 for an examination occurring before January 1, 2001, or $300.00 for an examination occurring after January 1, 2001.
2. The fee for applying for reexamination or recertification is $100.00 for a reexamination or recertification occurring before January 1, 2001, or $200.00 for a reexamination or recertification occurring after January 1, 2001.
3. The fee for admission without examination is $400.00 for an admission without examination before January 1, 2001, or $600.00 for an admission without examination after January 1, 2001.
4. The additional fee for late filing of application or transfer of an application is $100.00.

C. The supreme court, by administrative order or rule, may increase the amounts prescribed in subsection (2)(a), (b), or (c) within the following limits:

1. The fee for applying for an examination occurring after January 1, 2002 may be increased to not more than $400.00.
2. The fee for applying for a reexamination or recertification occurring after January 1, 2002 may be increased to not more than $300.00.
3. The fee for admission without examination after January 1, 2002 may be increased to not more than $800.00.

D. Each member of the board is entitled to receive compensation for his or her services, as are authorized by the supreme court and appropriated by the legislature, and in addition the actual and necessary expenses incurred in the discharge of his or her duties as a member of the board. The expenses of the board shall be paid upon certification by the supreme court pursuant to the procedures established by the supreme court.

Policy Statement

931-1. *Fees*

Fees must be paid by money order, cashier's check or certified check.

MCL 600.934 Qualifications for admission to bar; "good moral character" defined; election to use multi-state bar examination scaled score; disclosure of score.

A. A person is qualified for admission to the bar of this state who proves to the satisfaction of the board of law examiners that he or she is a person of good moral character, is 18 years of age or older, has the required general education, learning in the law, and fitness and ability to enable him or her to practice law in the courts of record of this state, and that he or she intends in good faith to practice or teach law in this state. Additional requirements concerning the qualifications for admission are contained in subsequent sections of this chapter. As used in this subsection, "good moral character" means good moral character as defined and determined under 1974 PA 381, MCL 338.41 to 338.47.

B. A person may elect to use the multi-state bar examination scaled score that the person achieved on a multi-state bar examination administered in another state or territory when applying for admission to the bar of this state, but only if all of the following occur:

  1. The score that the person elects to use was achieved on a multi-state examination administered within the 3 years immediately preceding the multi-state bar examination in this state for which the person would otherwise sit.
  2. The person achieved a passing grade on the bar examination of which the multistate examination the score of which the person elects to use was a part.
  3. The multi-state examination the score of which the person elects to use was administered in a state or territory that accords the reciprocal right to elect to use the score achieved on the multi-state examination administered in this state to Michigan residents seeking admission to the bar of that state or territory.
  4. The person earns a grade on the essay portion of the bar examination that when combined with the transferred multi-state scaled score constitutes a passing grade for that bar examination.
  5. The person otherwise meets all requirements for admission to the bar of this state.

C. The state board of law examiners shall disclose to a person electing under subsection (2) to transfer the multi-state bar examination scaled score achieved on an examination administered in another state or territory the score the person achieved as soon as that score is received by the board regardless of whether the person could have obtained that score in the jurisdiction in which the examination was administered. This subsection does not require disclosure by the board of the score achieved on a multi-state bar examination administered in another state or territory until the scores achieved on that examination administered in Michigan are released."

Policy Statements

934-1. *Good Moral Character*

See BLE Rule 2.

934-2. Transfer of Multistate Bar Examination Score

In some situations, applicants are allowed to transfer a scaled score from a multistate bar examination administered in another jurisdiction.

  a. That exam must have been taken within three years immediately preceding the exam the applicant wants to transfer the score to.
  b. The applicant must have passed the exam of which the MBE score the applicant seeks to transfer was a part.
  c. The jurisdiction from which the score is to be transferred must accept a Michigan MBE score for persons seeking admission to the bar of that jurisdiction. The other jurisdiction does not need to accept Michigan scores in every situation that Michigan accepts its scores, although if the other jurisdiction only accepts scores from concurrent examinations, Michigan will accept scores from that jurisdiction only from concurrent examinations.
  d. The essay answers of an applicant are graded and the combined score must constitute a passing score, regardless of the MBE transferred score.

934-3. *Timing of Request for Transfer*

Applicants are responsible for having information from another jurisdiction certified to the Board of Law Examiners. Applicants must notify the Board by mail—faxes and emails are not accepted—no later than May 15 for the July examination and December 15 for the February examination. This written notice of intent to transfer an MBE score is a necessary precondition to perfect the right to transfer an MBE score to Michigan.

MCL 600.937 General education requirements.

"Every applicant for admission to the bar is required to have completed successfully prior to commencement of his legal education at least 2 years of study, consisting of not less than 60 "semester hours" or 90 "quarter hours" of study in courses for which credit towards a collegiate degree is given, either in an accredited college authorized under the laws of the state in which the college is located to grant collegiate degrees, or in a junior college or other school from which students who have successfully completed such 2 years of study are accepted as regular third-year students by any accredited college in this state that is authorized by law to grant collegiate degrees."

Policy Statement

937-1. *General Education Requirements*

See BLE Rule 1.

MCL 600.940 Legal education requirements; military service.

    a.   Every applicant for examination is required to be a graduate from a reputable and qualified law school duly incorporated under the laws of this state or another state or territory, or the District of Columbia, of the United States of America.

    b.   If an applicant is called into or volunteers for the armed forces of the United States of America, and has completed successfully 2 1/2 years of the course of study as a fulltime student, or 3 1/2 years of the course of study as a part-time student, in any such law school, the board of law examiners, in its discretion may allow such applicant to be examined for the bar prior to such graduation, but shall withhold certification until after his graduation.

Policy Statement

940-1. *Reputable and Qualified Law Schools*

    See BLE Rule 2.

MCL 600.943 Examination of schools and colleges.

"The board of law examiners has the authority to examine, or to cause to be examined, any school, college, junior college, or law school for the purpose of determining whether the standards of education and training required for admission to the bar are being maintained, and to exclude from the bar examination any person who was a student therein at the time any such educational institution is found to have been disqualified or of questionable reputation. The board of law examiners may exclude from the bar examination any person who was a student in any such educational institution if such educational institution refuses to allow the examination."

MCL 600.946 Foreign attorneys; admission to bar, qualifications, extension of term.

"Any person who is duly licensed to practice law in the court of last resort of any other state or territory or the District of Columbia, of the United States of America, and who applies for admission to the bar of this state without examination, is required to prove to the satisfaction of the board of law examiners that:

    a.   He is in good standing at the bar of such other state, territory, or district, and has the qualifications as to moral character, citizenship, age, general education, fitness and ability required for admission to the bar of this state;

    b.   He intends in good faith either to maintain an office in this state for the practice of law, and to practice actively in this state, or to engage in the teaching of law as a fulltime instructor in a reputable and qualified law school duly incorporated under the laws of this state; and

    c.   His principal business or occupation for at least 3 of the 5 years immediately preceding his application has been either the active practice of law in such other state, territory, or district or the teaching of law as a full-time instructor in a reputable and qualified law school duly incorporated under the laws of this or some other state or territory, or the District of

Columbia, of the United States of America, or that period of active service, full-time as distinguished from active duty for training and reserve duty, in the armed forces of the United States, during which the applicant was assigned to and discharged the duties of a judge advocate, legal specialist or legal officer by any other designation, shall be considered as the practice of law for the purposes of this section, which assignment and the inclusive dates thereof shall be certified to by the judge advocate general or comparable officer of the armed forces concerned or by the principal assistant to whom this certification may be delegated; or any combination of periods of practice thereof. The supreme court may, in its discretion, on special motion and for good cause shown, increase said 5-year period. Any period of active service in the armed forces of the United States not meeting the requirements of duty in the armed forces as herein stated may be excluded from the 5-year period above prescribed and the period extended accordingly."

Policy Statement

946-1. *Admission Without Examination*

An applicant for admission without examination who has previously failed the Michigan bar examination will be referred to the Board by the Executive Director before the application is processed through the National Conference of Bar Examiners. Having failed the bar examination is not an automatic bar to admission without examination. See BLE Rule 5.

APPENDIX C

Research Resources

<u>Online resources</u> – this is just a sample of places you can search to begin the application process.

Social Security Administration

  http://www.socialsecurity.gov/onlineservices

  This site can tell you about previous jobs you held where SSI was drawn

Michigan Secretary of State   http://www.michigan.gov/sos

  This site can give you information where to get your driving record including history of where you lived while you were licensed as reported to SOS.

Michigan State Police   http://www.michigan.gov/msp

  This site can provide help in getting fingerprints and some criminal records

Internet Criminal History

  http://apps.michigan.gov/ichat/home.aspx

  Access Tool

  This site, found on the MSP site (above), can get a print out of your reported criminal history. It will indicate dates, courts involved, initial charges and final charges/convictions.

Internal Revenue Service   http://www.irs.gov

  This site can give you job history and some address history if you filed taxes.

State Bar of Michigan   **Http://www.michbar.org**

  This site has a lot of information regarding courts, names, addresses and contact info for judges, attorneys, government agencies, other states' bar associations as well as information on the application process.

Paid Services

Intelius   http://www.intelius.com

This is a paid site that can provide comprehensive information from the web on all matters found in the public record. This includes lawsuits, bankruptcy filings, voting records, address and phone histories, ownership of land and vehicles, etc.

Westlaw People Map   http://www.westlaw.com

For subscribers: this service is like Intelius in terms of looking up the entire public record on an individual.

Lexis-Nexis Comprehensive Person Search   http://www.lexis.com

For subscribes: this service is like Intelius in terms of looking up the entire public record on an individual.

APPENDIX D

SAMPLE EMPLOYER LETTER

October 55, 2028
District Committee Member, Esquire
Blah Blah Law firm
1313 Mockingbird Street Birmingham, MI 49999
    Re: Candidate
Dear Mr. Member:

We submit this letter in support of Candidate's petition for licensure and admission to the State Bar of Michigan. Mr. Candidate began working as a law clerk for our firm,_____, PLC, on April 38, 2023. During his employment with our firm, he has performed his work diligently and with commitment to the tasks assigned to him.

Mr. Candidate has been primarily involved in performing legal research on a variety of topics relating to our practice, an area of law with which he had no prior experience. However, despite this lack of experience, Mr. Candidate has embraced the assignments given to him, and spent long hours drilling down into the details of each factual scenario in conjunction with the terms and conditions of the applicable insurance policies. Each of the assignments given to Mr. Candidate have involved complex legal issues for which he has been required to learn and sift through voluminous case law and complicated factual scenarios regarding insurance coverage for claims ranging from copyright infringement to computer fraud to product liability coverage disputes. After completion of this legal research and investigation, Mr. Candidate has been required to reduce the results of his research into lengthy legal memorandums presented in an organized, thoughtful and logical fashion.

During his nearly five months of employment with our firm, Mr. Candidate has been punctual, hard-working, truthful, and earnest. He has accurately cited to authorities supporting his research and writing, and properly credited sources and authors on which he has relied. Further, prior to his employment with our firm, Mr. Candidate forthrightly disclosed to us the problems he created and/ or was involved in during law school and before. None of the matters in which he was previously involved have recurred during his employment with our firm, and there has been no indication that such problems are likely to recur in the future.

Please let us know if further information is needed or if you have any questions.

Thank you for your attention.

Sincerely,
Employing Law Firm

SAMPLE CHARACTER LETTER FROM FAMILY FRIEND

October 55, 2028
District Committee Member, Esquire
Blah Blah Law firm
1313 Mockingbird Street Birmingham, MI 49999

Dear Member:

We are writing this letter on behalf of Mr. Candidate

regarding his character and fitness to be recommended for admission to the practice of law in the State of Michigan.

We have known Candidate and his family for the past 20 years. Not only have we become extremely close to him, our families have maintained a close relationship through the years as well.

Candidate and our daughter Roxanne have been in a committed relationship for approximately three years. She is very ambitious and is extremely successful in her career. She has a definite plan for her life, one of which would not include someone who does not share the same goals and future aspirations.

Through the years, we have watched Candidate grow into a mature and responsible young man. He has consistently demonstrated to us to be dependable and has become someone we can trust in all aspects of our family life and in the relationship he has with our daughter.

Candidate is an honest young man with an excellent work ethic. We observed him throughout law school as being extremely conscientious and dedicated to his studies. In fact it was quite common for Candidate not to attend family functions because of the demands of the law program and his commitment to excellence.

We are aware Candidate is not perfect, but we feel confident that he has learned from his mistakes and has grown into an outstanding adult as a result of the lessons he has learned. We see time and time again, that often the individuals that make mistakes in their young lives turn out to be our best adults (citizens) and we believe that Candidate is one of those individuals. His determination is a result of his life experiences and ambition and desire to build his career and his future practicing law.

We believe that Candidate possesses the requisite character and fitness for admission to the Bar and we ask that you take into consideration the information that we have provided to you.

SINCERELY

SAMPLE LETTER FROM MEMBER OF SBM

October 55, 2028
District Committee Member, Esquire
Blah Blah Law firm
1313 Mockingbird Street Birmingham, MI 49999

Re: Letter of Recommendation Mr. Candidate

Dear Mr. Member:

I write this letter of recommendation on behalf of Mr. Candidate in relation to his admission to the State of Bar of Michigan. I have known the family, including Candidate, for over 20 years. I am a close family friend and have provided guidance to Candidate and his parents with regard to Candidate's unfortunate circumstance. Given my history with the family and Candidate, I believe my letter will assist you with your analysis as to whether Ted possesses the good moral character and general fitness to be a licensed attorney in the State of Michigan.

    a.   Unfortunate Events

Within a few months of receiving his pilots' license, Candidate was involved in a barnstorming accident that resulted in the death of a passenger. This accident was the situation we all worry about as passengers when our children have become new pilots. Candidate flew the plane in an unsafe manner making a mistake that many of us have made - unfortunately, his mistake had tragic consequences.

Candidate admitted his error and responsibility for the accident. He was charged criminally and had a civil suit filed against him and his parents. He pled details, details, details >>>>>>>>>>>>>>> >> >>> >>> >>> >>> >><>> judgment, which we all wish would have ended differently. He has expressed remorse and learned from it.

    b.   Lengthy description of recovery and reformation
    c.   Conclusion

Very Truly Yours, Joe Cool, Esq.

APPENDIX E

STATE OF MICHIGAN
IN THE SUPREME COURT
THE STATE BAR OF MICHIGAN

IN RE:

Applicant   Applicant No.:

_____/

TIMOTHY A. DINAN (P49499)

Dinan & Associates, P.C.
Attorney for Applicant
14950 E. Jefferson Ave., Suite 170
Grosse Pointe Park, MI 48230
(313) 821-5904

_____/

QUESTIONS TO ATTORNEY/EMPLOYER

1. Please state your name and current professional address.
2. What do you do for a living? How long have you been licensed as an attorney? Where do you work?
3. How do you know Applicant? How long have you known him/her? How often do you see him during the week?
4. What type of work does Applicant do in the office? Did you train him/her in any of his/her current work tasks? Do you supervise him directly or indirectly? Are you satisfied with his/her work and efforts? Does he work for anyone else in your office? Would you hire him/her to work in your office as an attorney if he/she receives his/her license?
5. Do you understand the issues that bring Applicant before this committee? How did you learn about them? When did you learn about these issues? Did his revelation of these issues change your opinion of him?
6. What is Applicant's reputation in your office for honesty? Intelligence? Productivity?
7. Do you have any concern that Applicant's conducts himself/herself in manner outside of the office that would be a poor reflection on you, your firm or our profession?
8. Have you ever had any concern that would lead you to recommend that he/she seek personal counseling or other professional assistance? Are you aware that Applicant is currently is in counseling?
9. Has anyone else in your office expressed concern for Applicant's ability to get his/her work done, arrive on time or other shortcoming that would make you question his/her abilities and character?
10. Do you believe that Applicant has the necessary character and fitness to practice law in MI? Why do you believe that?

STATE OF MICHIGAN
IN THE SUPREME COURT
THE STATE BAR OF MICHIGAN

IN RE:

Applicant   Applicant No.:

_____/

TIMOTHY A. DINAN (P49499)

Dinan & Associates, P.C.

Attorney for Applicant

14950 E. Jefferson Ave., Suite 170

Grosse Pointe Park, MI 48230

(313) 821-5904

_____/

<u>QUESTIONS TO ATTORNEY/FRIEND</u>

1. Please state your name and current professional address.
2. What do you do for a living? How long have you been licensed as an attorney? Where do you work?
3. How do you know Applicant? How long have you known him/her? How often do you see him/her during the week? How about when you attended law school? Do you still stay in touch with him/her?
4. Do you understand the issues that bring Applicant before this committee? How did you learn about them? When did you first learn about these issues? Did his revelation of these issues change your opinion of him? Do you know whether these incidents affected his reputation in law school? How?
5. Do you have any concern that Applicant's current conduct would be a poor reflection on our profession? Are you concerned the behavior he manifested in law school could arise in the future? Why not? Do you believe Applicant has the capacity to ask for help when he is in need?
6. Are you aware that Applicant has sought and still receives personal counseling? Do you believe it has been helpful? Why?
7. Do you believe that Applicant has the necessary character and fitness to practice law in MI? Why do you believe that?

APPENDIX F

STATE OF MICHIGAN
IN THE SUPREME COURT
THE STATE BAR OF MICHIGAN

IN RE:

Applicant   Applicant No.:

_____/

TIMOTHY A. DINAN (P49499)

Dinan & Associates, P.C.
Attorney for Applicant
14950 E. Jefferson Ave., Suite 170
Grosse Pointe Park, MI 48230
(313) 821-5904

_____/

QUESTIONS TO TREATING PROFESSIONAL

1. Please state your name and current professional address.
2. Please tell the panel briefly about your professional credentials.
3. How long have you been counseling professionally?
4. When did you first meet Applicant? Do you recall why he/she first came to your office? Are you aware of the specific reasons Applicant has been called before this committee?
5. How many times has Applicant seen you? Is that enough to establish a patient-therapist relationship so that you can render an opinion about him/her? How intensive is a two visit per week schedule in the spectrum of counseling treatment?
6. Did you develop diagnoses for Applicant? Can you explain how those diagnoses manifested themselves?
7. Was there an initial reluctance by Applicant to discuss the issues that brought him to your office? Can you describe how that manifested itself? Did he eventually open up to you? Do you believe he/she was and is forthright in his/her discussions with you in therapy?
8. Do you think Applicant recognizes the factors that led to his/her behaviors for which he/she is now before this committee? Given his/her participation in counseling with you, do you believe he/she has a better understanding of his environment, his family background and how these factors contributed to who he/she is?
9. Do you believe that Applicant recognizes the inappropriateness of his/her behaviors as you understand them? Is he/she likely to repeat such behaviors given his/her counseling experience? Why do you believe that?
10. Do you believe he/she will conduct himself in an ethical and forthright fashion in his/her professional and personal business?

APPENDIX G

STATE OF MICHIGAN
IN THE SUPREME COURT
THE STATE BAR OF MICHIGAN

IN RE:

        Applicant   Applicant No.:

_____/

TIMOTHY A. DINAN (P49499)

Dinan & Associates, P.C.
Attorney for Applicant
14950 E. Jefferson Ave., Suite 170
Grosse Pointe Park, MI 48230
(313) 821-5904

_____/

QUESTIONS FOR LAY WITNESS

1. How long have you known Applicant?
2. In what capacities do you know Applicant (family friend, employer)?
3. How would you characterize Applicant's participation in AA?
4. Does he/she contact you outside of meetings for support? How often?
5. Is he/she diligent in his participation and working of his/her steps?
6. Do you have an opinion regarding Applicant's intellectual abilities?
7. Do you have an opinion regarding Applicant's work ethic and dependability?
8. Does Applicant have coping skills to deal with the problems of others as well as his own?
9. Does Applicant share his/her concerns or problems with you?
10. Do you know if Applicant speaks with others about his concerns or worries?
11. Has Applicant discussed his/her past problems with you?

APPENDIX H

The Benefits of Including Psychotherapy in the Character & Fitness Process

There are significant benefits for both clients who have had their bar license challenged, as well as their representing attorneys, to obtain the assistance of a mental health professional when going through the Character and Fitness process. Psychotherapy is a tool which can shed some light on the reasons for clients succumbing to their transgressions initially, as well as provide some behavior modifications to put in place more positive coping skills and extinguish maladaptive behavior.

What Is Psychotherapy?

Psychotherapy is both an art and a science whereby a trained, licensed mental health professional interacts, usually through counseling, with one person or a small group of people for the purpose of evaluating, diagnosing, treating, and, hopefully, eliciting positive change in said people. Usually this change involves some combination of mental, emotional, spiritual, social, and/or behavioral growth, which sometimes can look or feel worse before it gets better. There are many different theories and schools of thought about how to accomplish this growth and the preferred treatment methods to get there – some even conflicting – just as there are several different categories of mental health practitioners depending on the type and length of their training. Of primary significance, however, is the relationship between the client and the therapist. It is commonly understood in the mental health field that, above and beyond the significance of most other components, if the therapeutic relationship between the client and the therapist "clicks," therapy will be successful. However, what makes this therapeutic relationship unique compared to other relationships in our lives is that there is actually no "relationship" as a layperson might understand it. The therapist is neutral and therefore is able to be witness to all sides of a person. The client and the therapist do not have a dual relationship or interact in any capacity other than in treatment. Also, the therapist ethically cannot benefit from the therapeutic relationship in any way except through monetary compensation – and, on a human level, perhaps a little pride or personal satisfaction about assisting the client in creating positive change in his or her life. The therapist, ideally, will be an objective observer and a mirror for the client, will be an advocate for the client, will challenge, support, sometimes comfort, and even briskly confront the client, yet maintain a professional distance with some perspective and unconditional acceptance. If a therapist is unable to achieve that for whatever reason, it is their professional obligation to refer the client out. In therapy there is definitely a delicate balance to maintain this boundary, especially because the therapist often must treat different clients differently based on the clients' issues, strength, and ability to be autonomous. Good therapists also make a conscious effort not to "put the client in a bell jar" or take a superior stance that disempowers the client, yet there should still be an ability to evaluate the client's growth and progress in treatment in a measurable, objective way.

Diagnostic Purposes for Therapist, Attorney, and Client

In the whole Character & Fitness process, a question that seems to come up repeatedly is "why?" – Why did a certain candidate do certain things, why does he or she behave in a certain way, and what is his or her diagnosis? Then, of course, the question is, what do we do now? And then, the inevitable follow up question remains: Is this maladaptive behavior going to continue, and hence, render the candidate unfit to practice law?

The inclusion of psychotherapy in the Character & Fitness process can be instrumental for a few different reasons. For the therapist, the client's participation in psychotherapy and how treatment evolves provides insight into the client's history, why the client did (or didn't do) certain things, and brings together the pieces of the client's life that previously would have made no sense or seemed disjointed. Over time a good therapist can gain a sense of the client's character, motivations, and behavioral tendencies. The therapist can help the client explore his or her history and past experiences to understand how that particular client ended up in the current state or situation. Again, different therapists come at this evaluation process from different perspectives.

This writer believes that each human being is born with some innate tendencies, strengths, and weaknesses. Each human being enters the world with these traits and, based on the conditions and circumstances that he or she faces and his or her ability to adapt, decides on certain ways of behaving in order to cope and survive. Most often we each continue to behave that way until it stops working. Usually once clients have come into the Character & Fitness process, they are starting to become aware that what they were previously doing is no longer working, and they are forced to push their comfort zone to make changes. This process may be met with resistance! Especially at first. Becoming aware of all of these pieces of the developmental process is key for the therapist to help the client see who they are and why they have behaved in the ways they have, why it is no longer appropriate, and how to adapt more appropriately in the present. Keep in mind that most people are not bad people, even if they behave in maladaptive ways. Each of us is just trying to survive and get our needs met. Hopefully we will get our needs met in positive ways, but, if not, we will get our needs met in maladaptive ways. Either way, however, we <u>will</u> get our needs met. It's all about survival.

Above and beyond people merely seeking to survive, however, there is a small segment of the population who really are very mentally ill, and where this serious pathology is the basis behind their maladaptive behavior. Chances are, someone who is organized and motivated enough to get through law school is less likely to be severely mentally ill as the people who sadly cannot "hold it together" enough to meet such long-term and complex responsibilities. However, there certainly are very intelligent, high-achieving, extremely sick people in influential positions who still manage to achieve some professional success and can be quite dangerous to themselves or others. This could include, for example, people who are psychotic (who have broken from reality) such as someone suffering from paranoid schizophrenia, or people who are sociopaths or have anti-social personality disorder (who do not subscribe to the mores of society and feel no remorse for their actions.) Certainly an advantage to having a client in psychotherapy is that they will be formally assessed by a mental health professional trained to determine the nature of the client's condition and how this might influence their Character & Fitness. Also, even with severe mental illness, it is possible for a client who is stable on medication, motivated and compliant in treatment, and managing his or her condition to function reasonably well as a professional. However, due to the serious nature of chronic and persistent mental illness, this must be evaluated by a trained mental health professional on a case-by-case basis.

The insight and understanding that a therapist gains about a client can be instrumental for the attorney defending the client in determining why a candidate did something and how to build a case around it. For this reason it would be important for the therapist to have the client sign a release so that he or she can confer with the defending attorney on a regular basis and coordinate care. Likewise, it is helpful in the therapeutic process for the therapist to know what the legal issues are and what challenges the client will face before the State Bar. The therapist must know why the client's transgressions were of issue for the Bar so the therapist can help the client gain insight. This will facilitate personal and professional growth for the client, and it will also be good preparation for the potentially grueling experience of testifying on his or her own behalf before a committee who may be very intimidating. If an attorney wants his or her clients to be as prepared as possible going into a hearing, one of the best training grounds is in a therapeutic setting where the clients can truly learn about who they are and "what makes them tick." Most people take years to know themselves without professional help. Even as the reader digests this text, are you able to identify your strengths and weaknesses? Your defense mechanisms? Your hurts from childhood that may still be affecting your life today? Hopefully you can. But if you struggle, imagine if your career were on the line while you struggled. We all have strengths, weaknesses and insecurities. But gaining understanding about these things is the difference between us managing our issues, versus our issues managing us.

As for the client, hopefully he or she will continue therapy long enough to start to see the benefits outlined above as they apply personally. There is usually a point during the therapeutic process where this writer can see a Character & Fitness candidate shift the motivation from the external ("I'm doing all this stuff in order to make those people happy and get my Bar license") to the internal ("I really appreciate knowing myself better and improving my life and my behavior – whether I obtain a Bar license or not.") To be able to look at history, at why maladaptive behaviors began, why such behaviors were destructive, and how to change those behaviors so they are more congruent with the client's values is a life-changing experience for a client, and essential for one going into the Character & Fitness process. At times it is assumed that highly educated, intelligent people have no need for deliberate self-reflection because it is seen as an unnecessary luxury or that they can be "successful" without it. This is not always the case. In our society, it seems that intelligence, knowledge, wisdom, and insight are terms often used interchangeably, when in reality they are not synonymous. A client may be very bright, have gone to a well-respected university, have graduated with honors and possess vast amounts of knowledge, even have a good deal of experience, but without insight into themselves and how they interact with the world, life will be difficult.

Rehabilitative Purposes for Client, Supplemental Support, and Coping

A candidate in the Character & Fitness process has been introduced into "the system" because he or she has been challenged by the State Bar, and there is a possibility that he or she will have a law license revoked or be prevented from obtaining one in the first place. This challenge resulted from an examination of behaviors not appropriate for a practicing attorney because the candidate's character has been called into question. Obviously, therefore, part of the therapeutic process will involve rehabilitating the client so that the pattern of old, maladaptive behaviors will cease and be replaced with behavior that the Bar determines to be reflective of good moral character, rendering the candidate fit to practice law. This successful rehabilitation is absolutely possible. However, it is the State Bar's job to be satisfied that such change has taken place and be sure it will persist without recidivism. The members of the review committee will not grant a Bar license if they have doubts.

Psychotherapy comes in, as outlined above, as the tool by which clients can know themselves better and learn how to get their needs met in more appropriate ways. There are certain common patterns of behavior that this writer has witnessed over time. Some candidates go before the State Bar with a history of misrepresenting themselves. Perhaps they have embellished something, or downplayed something so as to "bend" or "spin" the truth in their favor. Sometimes they have lied outright. Usually such behaviors are the result of insecurities more so than deliberately malicious attempts to deceive. I have heard many candidates admit that they desperately needed to "look perfect," and that they feared the truth would not be enough. Why that condition exists depends on the history of the individual client in question. The treatment, however, comes in discovering insights about the past and gaining the strength to make different, more candid, decisions in the future. Sometimes there is substance use involved that causes clients to compromise their judgment or behave erratically. Often substance abuse is a symptom of another issue the client struggles to cope with, and thus, wants to escape from, and then often substance abuse quickly becomes its own problem. Full-blown addiction is a chronic condition, yet with treatment, a recovering person can be symptom free. Other examples, such as belligerence, excessive spending, or other abdications of responsibility that make clients look as though they feel they are above the law, also require intervention by a trained mental health professional for best results of rehabilitation.

During the course of treatment a therapist is facilitating the client's work toward treatment goals that the client has drafted. Objectives that are behavioral and/or measurable can be tracked to show progress. Even if the client's gaining of insight is gradual, the progression in a positive direction should be evident. The therapist acts as a "coach" who helps a client in self-reflection and self-monitoring. The therapist is there for an extended period of time (at minimum, six months of regular participation in treatment) so that, in between sessions, as life happens, how a client responds to people and events can be discussed and evaluated so course corrections can be consciously implemented.

During this therapeutic process it should be openly discussed that the therapist acts as a support to the client and facilitates their accessing other supports in life as well. This would include responsible (and candid) friends and family members, a sponsor in Alcoholics Anonymous or Narcotics Anonymous, or other lifelines to help the client access true strength instead of using other, maladaptive means of coping with life. Ideally, clients will have a group of support persons available to them, including more objective individuals (like a therapist who operates from a professional distance) as well as trusted loved ones who are able to provide comfort or be called at 2:00 am if the clients should have such a need. Learning to access this support system is key as a means of helping clients to cope in healthier ways instead of acting out in their former, maladaptive ways – i.e, humbling one's self and honestly admitting insecurity to a friend in a phone conversation is far less destructive (and reflects far more strength) than pretending to be unaffected and covering the pain and becoming intoxicated. In psychotherapy, positive coping skills are created, taught, and practiced during the course of treatment, and discussions of how and why this change is successful and important help to concretize the significance of implementing this new behavior.

Parameters, Timeframe, and Limitations of Psychotherapy

The logistics of psychotherapy should be clearly explained. Each session, technically, is supposed to be about 50 minutes – to allow the therapist time to review a chart before a session and keep sufficient notes following a session. The reality is, most clients are unaware of this typically accepted time frame for the therapeutic "hour" that they assume is 60 minutes. In reality, it often seems almost too brief to accomplish enough. But with focused effort, a willing client, and a skilled therapist, a good deal can usually be accomplished during the 50 minute hour, and over time the client's progress becomes apparent.

A client absolutely must be able to build a relationship with the therapist for therapy to be successful. Usually a good therapist has several ways of establishing a connection with many types of people. But, within the human condition, sometimes the relationship just doesn't "click," and a professional should not be offended if the client requests a referral to another therapist. The key is for the client not to give up the search for a good fit. Once the therapeutic relationship has begun to be established, the therapist should spend some time reviewing the client's history with the client and assisting the client in drafting treatment goals in his or her own words. It helps for the therapist to consult with the referring attorney about what the Character and Fitness issues are. Over the first couple of months the client's underlying issues should naturally emerge in treatment as counseling peels the proverbial onion, and the ways to address those core issues can be woven into the treatment process.

Reasonable progress can be made gradually, over several months. This is one reason why, even though each client grows at his or her own rate, a certain amount of time simply has to pass in order for progress to be apparent and documented. If a therapist says to a new client, "12 sessions is usually the minimum requirement to constitute minimum effort in showing motivation and compliance," some clients will say, "Oh! So if I come twice per week then we can be done with all of this in six weeks?!" Well, not exactly. The point is to show reasonable willingness and participation, motivation and compliance, as well as to allow for sufficient time to pass for the client's growth to sink in and become more of a permanent change – therapists call this phenomenon "consolidation of gains." To cram a certain number of sessions into a small block of time might satisfy some quantitative requirement, but it really does not show that a person has changed. In fact, the very desire to rush through therapy shows only impatience and frustration with the limitations and requirements of the system, and not a true desire to improve one's self or address the bigger issue – what got the candidate into the system in the first place. It would be better for a client to participate in therapy once per week, or once every other week, for six months to a year, or sometimes more. That, at least, would show consistent effort and allow time for a stronger, more permanent transformation.

Some clients struggle to see their progress and may become discouraged with psychotherapy. When a very slow, gradual change is occurring over several months, periodic review of progress toward therapeutic goals helps. Also, this writer encourages clients to step back and examine their progress over time. Some sessions seem to be very enlightening and life-changing. Others might just feel like not much was accomplished. The human mind and heart are very complex things. Sometimes the window is open for change, and sometimes it is not. When all variables are in place in just the right way, amazing growth is possible. And there will most likely be certain "ah-ha!" moments, as we call them, when a client cannot believe they said or realized something that reflects growth and positive change. These are the stepping stones of insight.

At times clients are confused when they have been referred to multiple professionals. In the world of mental health treatment, it is typically considered to be a conflict of interest for a client to have more than one therapist. However, clients may require counseling by a psychotherapist, as well as medication management by a psychiatrist. Those two treatments can occur simultaneously and go hand in hand, and the clinicians involved should be conferring to coordinate care. Sometimes, also, LJAP (Lawyers and Judges Assistance Program) becomes involved and refers a client for substance abuse treatment with a professional in that specialty. This becomes somewhat more complicated, but it is possible for a client to see one clinician for substance abuse treatment and another for mental health.

This should be addressed openly with the client and, ideally, clinicians should be in communication with each other to coordinate care.

The additional advantage of clients participating in regular therapy for at least six months to a year is that the therapist has a reasonable amount of time not only to intervene in treatment, but to observe the growth of the client. This six month rule of regular sessions would constitute a minimum time line from which a therapist can establish character. The longer the client is in treatment, the more confident the treating clinician will be that their evaluations of the client are appropriate and accurate and the more consolidation of gains is apparent.

Psychotherapy does have its limitations, however. First, the client must be willing. If participation in treatment is driven solely by the State Bar's stipulations and external motivation of the client, or if such motivation persists as treatment progresses and the client never internalizes the benefits of counseling it will be more difficult. Second, the nature of the client's condition might be such that great transformation will not occur quickly. If the client presents with a personality disorder, brief therapy and/or medication alone will not suffice. In such situations, the client is on "the ten year plan" of consistent mental health treatment whether they like it or not, and the odds are good that, the very nature of the disease will prevent the treatment of it, and the client will not see the situation clearly or understand the ramifications. Clients also must fulfill other responsibilities that they may have in the community. It is one thing to explain why some behaviors have occurred by participating in insight-based work, but it is another level of responsibility entirely to make amends for past transgressions, make good on debts, correct past wrongs, and behave differently in the future.

Strengthening Credibility in Hearings

Introducing a psychotherapist into the Character & Fitness process often will have an overwhelmingly positive effect on the outcome. This is largely due to the huge growth in insight that the client will develop during the course of treatment. This writer has experienced several occasions where a State Bar committee demands to know why a candidate did or did not do something, or whether the candidate is likely to repeat, or not repeat, maladaptive behavior in the future. And, rightfully so, they are expecting a good explanation. Evaluation by a mental health professional and the resulting clinical work speak to the intent of the client in question to be rehabilitated and be willing to create a circumstance where a clinician can present a professional opinion about the progress a client has made. This strengthens the credibility of not only the client, but the representing attorney as well.

The intent of the therapist is to evaluate and rehabilitate the client, but also to represent that client in a way which hopefully will establish good character as it truly is (if it truly is,) and to present it in the real world. The therapist should help the client to open up, not just in therapy sessions to ferret out the core issues, but also in State Bar hearings, so that the committee can see any positive change before their eyes, as the truth really is. The more secure clients are with themselves, the less they will be "thrown off their square" by cross-examination. They will have nothing to hide, and hopefully, will be more comfortable with themselves, representing themselves as they truly are. Some of the most positive effects of successfully psychotherapy are the reflections of strength, genuine-ness, and humility in the client, as well as he or she taking responsibility for past transgressions. After all, clients can only be as honest with others (including the State Bar and their own attorneys) as they are with themselves. Psychotherapy helps clients get honest with themselves.

Find a Therapist Who Can Also Act As an Expert Witness

In the course of this Character & Fitness process, it is important that a candidate (or a representing attorney) find a psychotherapist who can also act as an expert witness. This means several things.

A good therapist to represent a Character & Fitness candidate would be someone who has good clinical skills and can evaluate, diagnose, and treat various conditions (or refer to specialists who can), and help the client gain insight into him or herself. A good therapist in this capacity also would shed light on clients' strengths and weaknesses, insecurities, defense mechanisms, survival skills, "character defects," and coping strategies, and be able to explain how this might influence the client's practice of law. A good therapist also would be able to help a client develop and demonstrate positive coping strategies in order to transform maladaptive coping skills into positive coping skills. A good therapist would be exceptionally articulate, both with oral and written language, as various types of communication are necessary to document progress with the State Bar. And, finally, a good therapist in this process would be able to testify with confidence before the Bar based on his or her experience, without being intimidated by seasoned attorneys or their cross examination, and he or she could shed light on how a specific candidate would be – or would not be - competent to practice law. A good therapist for this process could stand their ground and speak their mind clearly, directly, succinctly, respectfully, and without crumbling under pressure. Self-assuredness (without cockiness) is key.

Many psychotherapists – even ones experienced in their field - will admit to a fear of testifying due to a concern that they will be professionally discredited and "made a fool of" in public. A good expert witness obviously will be prepared for a potentially rigorous line of questioning and be able to maintain their composure and respond in an articulate fashion to deliver the truth.

There are many benefits to utilizing psychotherapy in the Character & Fitness process for both the client and the representing attorney. Evaluating the circumstances of a case, diagnostically determining what transpired in the past to cause the client to have his/her character and fitness challenged, and why, and rehabilitating the client are all advantages to including a psychotherapist in the case. Additionally, finding a therapist who can act as an expert witness and who can mentally and emotionally prepare the client would strengthen the credibility of the client, the attorney, and the case.